In the Hell of the Eastern Front

In the Hell of the Eastern Front

The Fate of a Young Soldier During the Fighting in Russia in WW2

Arno Sauer

Pen & Sword
MILITARY

An imprint of

FRONTLINE
BOOKS

Yorkshire - Philadelphia

FRONTLINE
BOOKS

Published in 2020 by Frontline Books,
an imprint of Pen & Sword Books Ltd,
47 Church Street, Barnsley, S. Yorkshire, S70 2AS

www.frontline-books.com

ISBN: 978 1 52673 333 7

For more information on our books, please visit
www.frontline-books.com, email info@frontline-books.com
or write to us at the above address.

Printed and bound by TJ International
Pen & Sword Books Ltd incorporates the imprints of Pen & Sword
Archaeology, Atlas, Aviation, Battleground, Discovery,
Family History, History, Maritime, Military, Naval, Politics,
Social History, Transport, True Crime, Claymore Press,
Frontline Books, Praetorian Press,
Seaforth Publishing and White Owl

For a complete list of Pen and Sword titles please contact
PEN & SWORD LTD
47 Church Street, Barnsley, South Yorkshire, S70 2AS, England
E-mail: enquiries@pen-and-sword.co.uk

Or

PEN AND SWORD BOOKS
1950 Lawrence Rd, Havertown, PA 19083, USA
E-mail: Uspen-and-sword@casematepublishers.com

For Father, whose experiences continued to encourage me
while writing this book.
For all future generations who have a right to the
truth about the past events.

After his training with the Reich Labour Service and the Wehrmacht eighteen-year-old Fritz is sent to Army Group North at the Eastern Front. There he has to fight for survival. He sees many of his comrades die. He himself receives a life-threatening injury. Yet that is not the end of his journey ...

Enthralling and unsparing, this is Arno Sauer's account of the true experiences of his father Fritz. Like his friends, he never wanted to be a hero and yet experienced at first hand what war really means. He and his fellow young soldiers were confronted with inconceivable suffering, and were always on the verge of death. His story is not least a powerful plea for peace.

Contents

Preface

For decades I have preserved in my memory the descriptions and accounts of the events that my father told me about his wartime experiences and youth during our countless Sunday walks in my childhood and adolescence. Often not voluntarily, upon my urging he recounted – sometimes only in fragments, but also for hours in great detail depending on his need and mood – experiences he lived through at that time; events and occurrences that moved, aggrieved and haunted him. Today I know that besides his ceaseless, exhausting work as master hairdresser with his own business my interest in his experiences helped him to come to terms with the bad memories and trauma of his youth.

It seems to me that it is now time for me to recount these past events, when immeasurable suffering and disaster took place. Crucial experiences like these must not be forgotten, and thus I wish to tell objectively how things were during these fateful years and how young people fared during that time.

Although innumerable publications exist on the Weimar Republic, the Third Reich and the Second World War, this authentic, objective and gritty story of a contemporary witness will reflect the life of the young generation and people in general at that time from their own perspective. Often, with the passage of time, this period of history has been distorted both positively and negatively; glorified and manipulated towards both ends. Therefore I wish to commit to historical memory and preservation the experiences of a boy from the Vordereifel, who is representative of a whole generation in the German Reich at that time.

Childhood, youth, apprenticeship, labour service, deployment as a soldier in a doomed, cruel war – a fate experienced in a similar manner by thousands of people – are all described in this biographical account.

It was a youth shaped in its foundations by its idealism and commitment, its enthusiasm, innovations, gullibility and morals, its decency and respect.

This was a generation that had to experience, suffer and bear a different kind of youth. Faced with growing up in a world that was crueller, harder and more desperate, bleaker and more disappointing, and full of hardship, they became more capable of suffering than many following generations. They were a gullible young generation cheated of their youth, betrayed and abused. They nonetheless never lost their courage or their faith in the good and in a better, more peaceful life.

No other country on earth had been so trodden to the ground in its total destruction after a long war more terrible and brutal than any previous war. The dire fact was that this calamitous conflict had emanated from German soil and after almost six years it ended there in absolute downfall.

A new beginning seemed more hopeless than ever, more difficult than in any other country afflicted by war. Thousands of cities, towns, villages, industrial installations, roads, bridges, churches, schools and hospitals had been destroyed. Five million soldiers had fallen or been reported missing, around 600,000 women, children and old people had fallen victim to uncounted bombing raids, up to two million people lost their lives while fleeing. More than 13 million people were driven from their former homeland in the German eastern territories.

The majority of these people did not give up and did not leave Germany. This also holds true for the poor expelled people and families from East and West Prussia, Pomerania, Silesia, Bohemia, Moravia and other German-speaking regions, who settled in the centre and west of Germany. They all stayed to rebuild Germany and to look forward in order to lead their country to a fair and better future, in spite of the inexpressibly severe and lasting suffering of many parties concerned.

This book shall contribute to the realisation that war does not only mean the worst for the people afflicted, but that such terrible, tragic events with all their consequences must be prevented before they reach that stage. It has been my intention to reflect the time then as it really was, without whitewashing or condemning, without glorifying or judging. All descriptions, even in their details, correspond to facts. Personal names have for the most part been kept in their original form except for the few that have been forgotten. Where required, in individual cases names have been changed to avoid distress for the relatives concerned.

Fritz was only twenty-one years old when the most horrible war of all time came to an end and he, like so many hundred thousands of other returning soldiers scarred in body and soul, had the great fortune to have escaped hell in order to see his beautiful homeland again and to return home. The events and experiences haunted him for the rest of his life with numerous nightmares, which however became less and less in the course of years and decades. The horrific images never left his thoughts entirely, though, and haunted him until the end.

There are no winners in war, only losers. Nothing stands above peace and the peaceful cooperation of all peoples and nations and their different religions.

Arno Sauer, Bassenheim,
January 2017

1
At the Reich Labour Service Model Camp, Moselle Region

On a gorgeous spring morning after the long, hard winter of 1940/41 the train brought me to the border with Luxembourg. When looking out from my third class-compartment with its uncomfortable, hard wooden benches I could admire the superb landscape passing by while in full bloom.

A few days earlier, four weeks after finishing my apprenticeship as a hairdresser, I had received the call-up order to the Reich Labour Service (Reichsarbeitsdienst = RAD). The official letter informed me that I would be deployed for one year to the 'model camp Moselle region' at Irrel and that I was expected there on time on the date given. So the evening before, besides some personal items, I packed the few things listed in the 'invitation letter' into an old small suitcase, and the next morning said goodbye to my mother and brothers with a heavy heart and marched to our train station.

The train journey first followed known routes to Mayen, where I had attended professional college, then onwards to Daun, Gerolstein, Kyllburg, Bitburg and on to Irrel. I – just seventeen years old – travelled for free, but with an uneasy feeling of uncertainty towards a destination that I had not chosen and that I did not want to visit.

With every kilometre farther from home a strange kind of disquiet grew inside me, mixed with homesickness. Not even the bread and dripping helped, which my mother had made for me at the last moment, and which I now ate with little appetite. Many thoughts, memories and instances of my not very lengthy past rolled past me like a film. I remembered my short adolescence and so many pleasant and sad occasions, for example the early loss of my father, who now could only accompany me on all my paths in my thoughts and in my heart. At just seventeen I now had to meet the demands of the regime during wartime, and these were harsh. Complaining and crying were not options for us, and insubordination could even cost you your life. It only remained for me to look ahead, to remain alert and to 'hear a pin drop' in the truest sense of this saying. It was important for survival for me to prepare myself without fear for situations that may arise suddenly and without warning.

While I mused about past incidents accompanied by the monotonous travelling sound of the railway wagons, I thought back with a smile to a story that, thanks to my brother Karl, had been decided in my favour at the last moment. While in our younger years Karl had always been bested by me during our scuffles in the farmyard or in the barn, I had no chance against him beyond the age of fourteen. Karl's enormous physical strength did not entice me to further trials of strengths.

I still recall vividly that Mother complained one day that the chickens in the barn were hardly laying any eggs any more, and she suspected the loss to be chiefly the work of a marten. After many weeks the 'marten' was finally caught, yet it turned out to have only two legs and was called Karl – it was my brother. For a long time the young, rapidly growing boy had been eating ten to twelve eggs a day in secret and without being discovered by sucking them raw. He was always hungry and the sweet egg yolk tasted particularly nice to him. Yet it was not only the many eggs, but also our fresh cow's milk, the additional bacon and the extra spoon of lard during lunch that led to our Karl becoming so strong. I on the other hand did not like fat, so that my share ended up on my brother's plate. Yet certainly our genetic disposition and most of all hard physical labour on our farm from an early age had played an important role, too.

Why do I mention this? One afternoon I was playing handball on the sports ground with the other boys. That went swimmingly until all of a sudden two slightly older players wanted to steal my ball because they envied my superior technique and were angry about the lost game. When they wanted to escape with it, we got into a scrap, during which my chances seemed very low. Still, during the scuffle another player ran to our house and fetched our Karl, who came to the aid of his brother. Although my two opponents were much older than him, he roughed them up without a problem, so that I had a lucky escape with just some scratches and, even saved my beloved ball.

The screeching brakes of the steam locomotive when arriving at Bitburg station plucked me from my thoughts back to reality. Now it was not long, and I faced the future events with optimism. I do not want to claim that I saw them as a pleasant new challenge for which I was longing. On the contrary, I would have liked to have stayed at home with Mother and pursue my profession as a newly minted journeyman. Yet at that time all my contemporaries and older young men were on the hoof far away, drafted into the Wehrmacht, in military training or at the front.

I accepted this new challenge and went on my way together with many other comrades of my age whom I had already met during the outbound journey on the train. We all had the same marching orders, and thus we marched together from the train station in Irrel to pass through the gate and past the guards at the camp at the appointed time.

After a short induction, after which we received our uniform, equipment and the famous spade, symbol of the Labour Service, we took quarters in one of the numerous barracks. Each dorm housed twenty men in ten bunk beds. Two of us shared one locker.

From now on we were woken daily at 5am by loud shouting. On the first day we began with early morning exercise. Afterwards we jogged stripped to the waist across the parade ground to the wash rooms. Then the cleaning of the dorm and precinct was scheduled, where we learned very fast in an unambiguous and clear manner what we needed to do. This was followed by breakfast, which was always a very meagre affair and had the consequence that hunger was our steady companion.

This was not altered by second breakfast at 9am either, as most of the time there was nothing left for us to eat. Only occasionally a few stale slices of bread were left over from breakfast, which we devoured greedily.

On the second day we had our medical examination to ascertain our fitness for duty and we were all declared fit. Also some Luxembourgian comrades, who lived just a few kilometres away on the other side of the Sauer River, performed their labour service with us. These boys were naturally even less enthusiastic than us, and our motivation was rather low, too. I found the Luxembourgian language with its singing intonation rather pleasant. Since we also spoke a dialect, the so-called Moselle Franconian, we could communicate well with each other.

The medical examination was carried out by a junior doctor with the rank of a lieutenant, and it was done quickly: height, weight, bending down once, a few notes, and finished.

General duty then began, which took on the same form for several months. There was early morning exercise every day and in all weathers. Sometimes we had a second set of exercise in the afternoon or evening. This was right up my street, since I loved sports and hence could also indulge in my hobby during Reich Labour Service.

Furthermore, there were daily lessons. These consisted of course of maths, German, geography, ethnography and music, but also of elements of National Socialist ideology such as racial studies. We also received training as paramedics and in weapons theory and topography. This was followed by a kind of military basic training where we learned military behaviour and precise marching. After we had rehearsed a few songs, we even marched singing. To this was added drill with the spade, which hardly differed from the later drill with the Carbine 98, the standard rifle of the Wehrmacht. For this we had to report to the parade ground, looking east. When the rising sun was reflected in 240 polished spades during presentation, this was a grand spectacle. The intention of this drill was unmistakable in so far as we had to work every day on the Siegfried Line with its wide network of ditches and bunkers that were being constructed in this region. We spent our time shovelling, digging, picking, moving soil, cementing and so forth. We had to carry out extremely exhausting work, and these physical exertions were asked of us despite us just having poor and not always sufficient food, as mentioned above.

I always viewed sports and formal education as a welcome diversion, and even the extremely harsh training did not dampen the mood. On the contrary, the atmosphere among us youngsters of the same age was really good considering the circumstances.

We learned quickly to enjoy small freedoms and how to shirk when the occasion arose. We also had the experience that our cohesion grew with the difficulties. We also learned quickly to stand up for each other in tricky situations. Hereby it was insignificant from which social class the comrades came or which professions they held. Whether baker, butcher, hairdresser, painter or smith; whether cobbler, chimney sweep, bricklayer or carpenter; whether roof tiler, joiner, farmer, labourer or A-level student – we respected each other without any prejudice. This was the guarantee for our comradeship. Cooperation bound us together into a clannish team, especially when the pressure of training and of the achievements expected from us were high. This spirit of comradeship would stand its test time and again in the worst possible situations at the front.

As a rule everyone could trust everybody blindly apart from a few odd-balls, who I also encountered during the war – not frequently, but every so often on. They were weirdos who were simply different than the others. Among them were lads who stood out conspicuously, who were dirty and unwashed, who excelled in shirking during cleaning the dorms and precinct or left the toilets in an unmentionable state, who fumbled when tidying the locker or during inspections of our attire or undermined our comradeship in an egotistical manner.

The victims of such behaviour were, in some cases, all of us, of course. This could mean an earlier wake-up call at 4am or even 3am, longer duty in the evening, a curfew at weekends and the loss of other privileges. Consequently it was quite possible that after any kind of unwelcome incidents the person in question was visited at night by the so-called 'Holy Ghost', and these serious or less drastic punitive measures contributed to discipline being better maintained. This action was not necessarily linked with pain, although for example removing black shoe polish from one's genitals could cause a discomforting reddening. Yet, as I said before, these comrades were far and few between.

The stricter and more humiliating the training was during the first weeks, the more life affirming we rose up again as a consequence, strengthened in body, spirit, and foremost in self-assurance. Conscious of our ability to cope and to suffer within this sworn brotherhood, even unpleasant situations could not shake us, as we experienced them from time to time with many a spiteful trainer.

We encountered these so-called 'sons of bitches' every so often, but they were not the rule. In general we experienced treatment that was disciplined and strict, but also humane and decent. I encountered nice people, both among the trainers and the comrades. In Paul Seidenfuß, a butcher's journeyman from Coblenz who had been drafted the same day as me, I found a reliable friend. We had much fun together and stuck to each other through thick and thin.

After twelve weeks the duty was loosened in so far as we received permission to leave on Sundays and holidays, if there was not a curfew at short notice due to some new watchwords or operations. Thus we explored Irrel, the Irrel waterfalls at the River Prüm and we sometimes wandered the few kilometres towards Luxembourg. At the former Reich border we reached the old border bridge of stone via the state road, which led us across the Sauer River to the little, cosy town of Echternach in Luxembourg.

On days without leave I used every occasion to pursue additional sports. I also had fun styling the hair of some comrades with a newly learned and extremely fashionable cut. This meant in practical terms: the sides extremely short and on the top long and combed back. This was considered the height of fashion at that time, and everybody wanted, of course, to emulate the ideal of handsomeness – especially if there was to be a dance in town, which we visited in uniform, where we enjoyed the covert glances of many a girl of the Federation of German Girls [Bund Deutscher Mädel = BDM] waiting to be asked to dance. None of us would at that time have come up with the idea to sport a bald head or a buzz cut as it was worn by Russian soldiers. In our eyes this looked unprepossessing and ugly. Only prisoners and old men wore their hair like this in Germany at that time. Yet this minimalistic hairstyle awaited many of us in later years, if we were lucky enough to survive the war and had the misfortune to end up as prisoners of war of the Allies. Yet none of us considered that possibility then, during this first half of 1941. Nobody had an inkling of what was in store for us.

Our comrade Franz Färber used his free time in a different manner. He was a genuinely gifted amateur artist and knew how to render faces absolutely true to life. Thus he made simple pencil sketches of some of us. I suffered through holding still for a long time, and my portrait was ready after two sessions with extensive cigarette breaks.

On 22 June 1941, the attack of the German Wehrmacht on Russia, Operation *Barbarossa*, named after the German emperor Friedrich I Barbarossa, began. The operation was launched from East Prussia in the north to the Carpathian Mountains in the south and involved three army groups, two air fleets and 2.5 million soldiers.

We learned this from our trainers in the classroom and reacted with embarrassed silence. There were no expressions of joy and no shouts of 'Hooray', as we had not thought that the military leadership would add another theatre of war to the existing ones. What would this mean for us? Why must this happen? Which purpose did this reckless, even crazy adventure serve? We were unable to make head or tail of this, just seventeen years old here at the Reich Labour Service camp not far from the border to Luxembourg. We could only accept this extremely disturbing news in silence, yet we sensed that something very threatening now approached us. During the next days and weeks we followed as if in a spell the reports on the radio and in the newspapers carried by euphoria and confidence in our victory. One victory report followed another in quick succession.

When the German attack stalled for the first time amidst the autumn mud and came finally to a total standstill a few weeks later shortly before Moscow due to a particularly early and bitter onset of winter, we received after eight months' duty in the Reich Labour Service ten days of leave shortly before Christmas. We had waited longingly for this time for a while, and I cannot describe the joy we felt when we boarded the train in Irrel to travel home for the first time after a long absence. The few letters I had received from Mother could not alleviate my homesickness and could not replace my home. Now finally the moment had come, at last!

Paul and I intended to travel on the same train, of course, and chose the connection via Trier-Ehrang, then Wittlich and along the lovely Moselle, past Cochem to Coblenz. Winter had covered the whole landscape with snow, and we enjoyed the passing romantic wintry landscape of the Moselle valley in a heated second class-wagon.

It was the third Christmas of the war and presents were scarce and paltry accordingly. Oranges and other tropical fruits had not been available for a long time, and coffee, flour, sugar and even shoes were rationed and only available with coupons, like many other items. It was quiet in our snowed in village. Life here seemed to stand still. Outdoor labour could no longer be carried out due to the extremely cold temperatures and heavy snowfall. Private motor cars no longer existed, and thus none were driving along the Reich road. Small children looked forward to tobogganing. We, however, were suddenly no longer children at seventeen years of age.

We had much time to think, and my thoughts often wandered back to my childhood and youth. I was born in Bassenheim near Coblenz in the Rhincland on 22 December 1923, five years after the end of the First World War, as the third son of the farmer and potato dealer Josef Sauer and his wife Antoinctte (née Quirbach, 1883). I was baptised in the Catholic parish church of St Martin's as Friedrich Gottfried.

The name Gottfried came from my godfather, a brother of my mother. As far as I can remember, the name Friedrich was never used in full, but I was exclusively Fritz, or 'dat Fritzje', as the Moselle Franconian dialect would have it.

My eldest brother Hans, actually my half-brother, was born in 1908 and for ten years lived alone with my mother with Mother's uncle Johann in rather poor conditions, after a young man from Saffig, roughly four kilometres away, had got my mother pregnant but then abandoned her despite his promise of marriage in order for him to emigrate to the USA.

When my father Josef Sauer (born 1880) in 1918 returned home unharmed after four years of war at the Western Front having received three decorations, whose meaning I was later unfortunately no longer aware of, he soon married my mother and adopted little Hans. He not only gave him his name, but always treated him like his own son. It was decided very early on that Hans, as the firstborn, and as was common in the Rhineland just as in most of the regions of Germany, ought to carry on our agricultural holding.

My second brother, Peter, was born in November 1920, and in May 1925 Mother gave birth to my third brother, Karl, when she was forty-two years old. In our village were many families who bore the same family name as us, and with few exceptions all of them only had male descendants. So my parents, who would have liked to have also a little girl, decided in view of my mother's advanced age not to have any further children. Economic aspects did not play an unimportant role in these considerations, either. After the lost war, during the years of the Weimar Republic, which were shaped by inflation and unemployment, for many people it was not possible to feed a large family adequately, let alone to equip them with the items required for a normal lifestyle.

If families after the founding of the Second Reich in 1871 had on average six to twelve children in the aspiring empire, this number sank by half after the First World War, so that the decrease in births was partly compensated for by the lower infant mortality. For not only medicine, but also the social system made revolutionary progress to some extent after the turn of the century. In particular hygienic conditions improved, and thus the number of deaths by infections was reduced drastically.

My parents both had seven siblings each, which meant an enormous number of cousins for me, with whom it was great to play. A special example of this was my uncle Peter Paul, a brother of my father. His family lived a few houses away in our street. Their house, built at the same time and of the same size, did accommodate a few more souls, though. Here still existed a truly extended family with eleven children, six boys and five girls. So in our village, besides Christmas, Carnival, Easter and the parish fair there were also numerous smaller family festivities, albeit of very modest proportions with regards to financial and culinary efforts.

In general there was always something happening in our village thanks to the many children – on the mostly still gravel roads, in the gardens, meadows, fields or in our beautiful woods. And so, if Father did not take us along to field work, we trekked and roamed through the village and its surroundings in the years before we were sent to elementary school, always looking for discoveries, an interesting distraction, adventures or just for something edible. From May to October we always knew where the first strawberries, raspberries and cherries or the last blackberries, plums, pears, nuts and apples were to be found.

Not far from our house in Von-Oppenheimer Street No. 1 was the well-paved Reich road. This led from Coblenz via Metternich, Rübenach, Bassenheim, Ochtendung, Mayen, past the Nürburgring completed in 1927, via Blankenheim, Schleiden, Monschau to Aachen. Here we could admire the passing cars, of course, which increasingly drove through our munici-pality in later years during the great Eifel races, especially during the Grand Prix of Germany. Yet automobiles were still rather rare at that time.

The Reich railway was the common mode of transport, and so the Reich road was as a rule more used by teams of horses and oxen, some trucks and pedlars, tinkers and basket weavers, travellers and other folk. At that time many journeys were still undertaken on foot and thus the motor enthusi-asts from our village walked the 41 kilometres to the Grand Prix on the Nürburgring, where such famous manufacturers as Auto Union, Mercedes-Benz, Alfa Romeo, Bugatti and Ferrari fought fierce battles with each other.

I can still very well remember an event of an entirely different nature. Barely six years of age, still before starting elementary school, I discovered gypsies who passed through our village coming from Ochtendung. That was, of course, thrilling. These people looked different, wore different kinds of clothes, spoke differently, and they had many children with them and a small shaggy horse, the like of which we had never seen in our village before. It was probably a kind of pony, which pulled a little smoking hut on two wheels. My curiosity was suddenly awoken, and seconds later I was sitting inside this vehicle. The people were friendly and merry. An elderly woman smoked a long pipe and while playing with their children for a time I forgot to hop off. Having jumped on at the entrance to our village, I suddenly saw our train station passing by, which was located far from the edge of our settlement on the opposite, eastern side. Now my courage suddenly left me. I jumped as quickly as possible from this fascinating vehicle leisurely making its way to Coblenz. When I was running away I saw that the jolly company had grown by a few chickens and a goose. The two kilometres walk back to our village and my house I managed easily and in the shortest of times. Walking or jogging was no problem for us.

Meanwhile, word had travelled around the village that little Fritzje had been taken along and abducted by the gypsies. They were looking for me everywhere and were in great distress. That I had voluntarily climbed onto the wagon out of curiosity, I kept to myself in view of the scolding I received when returning home. Immediately my parents searched my cropped hair for lice, but fortunately did not find any.

Due to the fact that I had been born late in December 1923, my enrolment in the Bassenheim elementary school only took place in Easter 1930 for those born in 1923/24. Enrolment always took place after Easter, not like today after the summer holidays. After the Easter holidays the new school year began, if one did not go to secondary school or began an apprenticeship. Elementary school then consisted of eight grades, hence eight years of school. Whoever was under-performing and could not cope with the subject matter had to simply repeat the grade.

Our elementary school was located on Saffinger Street, immediately above our beautiful castle grounds. Naturally all students went to school on foot, even those from the farms surrounding our area and from the houses around our rather faraway train station. I was lucky, as my home was only 500 metres from our school.

In short, we lived in a picturesque village embedded in the surrounding landscape and nature, virtually in paradise, if it had not been for the harsh life full of privations and labour in economically difficult times. Admittedly, our infrastructure had been significantly improved thanks to the newly established railway line that ran Coblenz–Mayen–Daun–Gerolsteine, to which our municipality was linked by a new and large train station. This also engendered a modest economic boom.

Even so, our municipality, dominated by farming, was markedly poorer in comparison to its neighbours Ochtendung, Mülheim, Kärich, Saffig and Kettig, although our district was significantly larger. Besides the classical skilled trades such as baker, butcher, hairdresser, blacksmith, carpenter, cobbler, tiler, plumber or joiner, there was a more than average number of families in our village who predominantly lived off agriculture, and without exception the land holdings of the farmers were rather modest. There was a simple reason for this: Bassenheim had since the early Middle Ages been under the rule of the Knights Walpot von Bassenheim, a famous, influential and wealthy knightly dynasty that received in the eighteenth century the rank of imperial count. This entailed an expensive maintenance of court whose costs had to be borne by the tenants of the various holdings owned by the noble house. In this manner the noble lords and ladies amassed a princely fortune in the truest sense of the word, while their subjects barely had enough to live on. This wealth can still be seen today in form of the beautiful castle, to which not only belongs a large park and several lakes, but also 1,000 hectares of forest and 1,000 hectares of fertile agricultural land including three farmsteads with forestry enterprise.

Everyday life for children and adolescents of my age was modest and full of work. Yet now and then we used self-invented distractions that we managed to make exciting.

As a rule we went to school every day just like normal. If there were tasks at home or on the fields, we had to help out. Whether we wanted to or not was of no interest to anybody. Most of the time we did not want to and would have preferred playing in the village, the forest, the meadows or our sports ground. The potato harvest was particularly laborious. Then these crops still had to be picked up by hand while bent down, and the sacks weighing 50 kilograms had to be lifted, which was rather difficult for us children.

I still hear my father today saying: 'Fritzje, if you diligently "hog" [lift] potatoes, then you will have a new pair of trousers for Christmas.' The next year it was new shoes. I would have needed new trousers and shoes anyway, and I believe that I would have got them from my parents even without 'hogging' potatoes.

Christmas was very festive, the presents in contrast rather modest. Unfortunately my birthday was on the 22nd as well. So these presents were combined with the Christmas gifts for simplicity's sake, which did not mean an increase, however.

In later years we knew, of course, that not Father Christmas, but our parents gave the presents. Nonetheless, our Hans continued to play Farmhand Rupert and threw a few handful of nuts, apples and even oranges through the open kitchen window into the house. To these were added the promised trousers or a pair of new shoes, further socks knitted by Mother and a bar of chocolate.

To come back to the potatoes once more, I would like to mention that their cultivation was the main income of our enterprise and thus crucial for our subsistence. As mentioned above, the Bassenheim farmers owned little land themselves, due to the large manorial estate, but often large families had to eke out a living from it. We owned eight acres, which amounted to just two hectares and was actually not much so we leased additional acres from the Catholic church.

As my father had kept a cow, chickens and pigs besides cultivating potatoes since the mid-twenties, we could live tolerably well and even afford two splendid horses. At that time many other farmers still had to do their field work with only one horse or with oxen and cows, so we considered ourselves lucky. The horses were not only employed for field work, but also for marketing and transporting our potatoes to our customers. These lived mainly in Coblenz and its surroundings.

This went relatively smoothly and as follows: during the day the potatoes were harvested and in the evening made ready on our cart in the farmyard. If business was booming, we bought additional potatoes from other farmers. During the night, between 2am and 3am, Father or my brother Hans got up, hitched up one of the horses, and the journey to Coblenz commenced, where they arrived very early. In the square Am Plan they halted at the horse trough. The horse received its nosebag and could quench its thirst. Subsequently the potatoes were delivered to the customers, who predominantly lived in the old part of town. We sold both to restaurants and private customers.

Our cart could be varied in its length. In its short variety we could transport up to twenty-five 50-kilo sacks. For delivered potatoes we received two Reichsmark more per 50 kilograms than normal marketing yielded. This was for us an enormous income of an additional 50 Reichsmark per trip. After word had got around of our quality and reliability, our orders became more extensive, and we could deliver larger quantities. For this purpose we extended our cart, i.e. pulled it apart like an extending table. That meant that we could now transport forty 50-kilo sacks, and the additional income increased thus to 80 Reichsmark per trip.

For the larger and heavier load, however, both horses had to be hitched up, as one horse alone could not pull the heavy cart over the incline of the Coblenz Road up to the hill at our train station. From there the route for the remaining 12 kilometres was level or even had a slight decline until the town centre. Yet since one horse was needed the next day for field work and Father needed his sleep for the heavy labour, I was woken at night by Hans. After all, I only needed to go to school the next day!

Thus, when eight years old I got up at 2am, hitched up the horses together with my brother and on we went. After two kilometres we reached the top of the hill, one of the horses was unharnessed, and I rode back home on this horse. I found it totally thrilling to ride all by myself through the pitch black of night at that young age. Except for the clip-clop of the horse's hooves, no further sounds were heard in this lonely silence. Only the twinkling stars and the moon were our companions during those nights. Nevertheless, I felt no fear. Rather, I was overcome by an elevated and proud feeling, because such a precious animal was entrusted to me. Only years later I became aware how consistently our parents raised us in the spirit of responsibility and commitment.

After arriving home, I first looked after the animal and then quickly returned to bed until the wake-up call. Of course, I did not need to get up every night. On some occasions it was my older brother Peter's turn, sometimes we had no extra orders. Yet when there were school holidays, I was almost always allowed to accompany the potato transports to town. This was, of course, an adventure for me. I left our village for the big, wide world – in my eyes at that time.

In Rübenach and still more so in Metternich, the houses became larger and more splendid. The most beautiful and largest villas in Metternich showed the years 1908 to 1913 on their facades. In this final phase before the First World War the economy had been booming, and many citizens had become rich. Farther we drove through the Coblenz district of Lützel with its splendid art deco houses, then over the Balduin bridge originating in the fourteenth century across the Moselle river into the historic part of town. Into town the old castle was on the left and opposite on the right side the Bassenheim Court with the neighbouring Dominican church.

'Lützel' in the Rhineland dialect incidentally means the same as the Northern German 'Lütje' i.e., 'little', which explained the proportions of the district in comparison to the opposite larger town. Then we turned into the old moat and drove until the aforementioned square, the so-called 'Plan' in the heart of the historic town. Here the delivery of our goods began, and I could observe how hard Hans had to work as he had to carry the 50-kilo potato sacks into the basements, but also up to the fourth or fifth floor of the large houses.

In between we fortified ourselves with a piece of pork sausage from a butcher and some slices of dark rye bread we had brought from home.

Although my task was to look after the horses and to assist in unloading, I ate just as heartily. Mother liked eating grapes and tropical fruits very much, which were only rarely available in our village, and so we bought her grapes and a few oranges, if the opportunity arose.

My big brother Hans was often extremely jolly towards the end of our delivery tour around noon. He began to sing and became more and more funny and merry. The origin of his good mood was easy to guess, as one could smell it from afar. At most delivery addresses Hans received a tip, which at that time often did not consist of cash, but rather was paid in kind. This in turn almost always took the form of alcohol such as beer, spirits such as schnaps, pomace brandy, cognac and similar, which was poured in thanks for Hans when he was sweaty and thirsty after carrying the heavy load the numerous stairs up to the attics or down to the basements. Polite and charming, as Hans was to all customers, he naturally could not resist the many treats. So there were some days on which Hans became drunk in a very short period of time.

The drive home then took a very leisurely form. Because the horses knew the way home, they trotted the route back on their own. If while we were in Metternich a tram – called generally the 'electric' in colloquial speech – approached from behind and rang its bell, the horses cantered away from the tracks automatically and as a matter of course. Such things often remained unnoticed by us, for I used to nap for a while on the journey and Hans slept off his drunkenness. Once the 'electric' had passed, the horses automatically returned to the lane and our journey continued without problems. Having reached the Bassenheim train station, the world was back in order. All troubles and labours were forgotten, and together we had managed an eventful day well.

On another day it might happen that Mother gave us the commission to drive the cart into the forest in order to collect wood and bundles of sticks. The latter served as tinder for the daily cooking or heating in the kitchen. The stove in our small living room was usually only heated during the winter, at Christmas or on other festive occasions. Another time the commission was to drive to any field plot where an apple or pear tree was just bearing fruits.

It was enough to drive you up the wall, since we children wanted to play and actually do quite different things. Yet it was not too bad for us children with respect to work. We still had enough leisure time, since school did not burden us too much with homework. During the warm season we went to the sports ground, and in wintertime we tobogganed or held snowball fights.

Especially during the winters of the 1930s or '40s of the last century, which were extremely heavy in snow, very cold and moreover very long, we spent days riding our sleighs from the Ochtendung or Saffing hill. There were, after all, hardly any cars on the roads. As a result the sledge runs were enormously smooth and very long. All children from the village, boys and girls alike, were on their feet, and the hills were teeming due to the large families with many children.

Most of the time several sledges were bound together. At the front a navigator wearing ice skates was placed. The runs were nevertheless adventurous. There were no lifts, of course, and the heavy sledges were dragged by hand to the starting point, and on some days more than 20 kilometres were covered in the snow in that manner.

I particularly enjoyed throwing snowballs, and therefore on various occasions the following incident happened due to my high spirits. Opposite our house, on the corner Von-Oppenheimer Street and Karmelenberger Way, stood the house of the Nachtheims. Here two childless spinsters were living together with their brother, who were always a little bit funny and odd and did not like us children in general. Naturally we enjoyed annoying these ladies from time to time, especially as they were so pedantic and touchy. I could aim quite well and hard, and in order to achieve the desired effect, I made a few water-hardened snowballs with a big pebble at the centre of each. If I stood on our outside staircase, I could fire a few of these rock-hard prepared 'full metal jackets' onto the closed wooden shutters at ten metres' distance over our high wooden gate.

This made a terrible racket, and my success rate was 100 per cent. I had just time to duck behind our high wooden gate, when the shutters flew open and the women screamed and shouted with shrill voices down our street: 'Down there the lad is running, down there the lad is running, police, stop him!'

I was in stitches, so that the following day I repeated this process a few times for my entertainment. It was a good thing that Father did not notice anything as this could have led to a really sound flogging. Fortunately it never came to light that I was the culprit.

At least these memories could cheer me up, as with the outbreak of the Second World War the mood in the village became extremely dismal. Many men were at the front, and some had already fallen. As a consequence, Christmas Mass in our parish church St Martin's was crowded to bursting point on Christmas Eve. It was very solemn and sad, as our country was amidst a war of uncertain outcome. None of us and of the village population had wanted it and many were wondering how our people, our country, might have got itself into this unforeseeable conflict. Only a few people realised the reason for Hitler's criminal politics, and these kept their mouth shut, since they would have risked liberty and life. During the song 'Silent Night' many tears were falling. Peace on earth was shattered, and the sense of this carnage probably only revealed itself to the fanatic supporters of the NSDAP. And there were not many of those in our village of just about 1,700 souls. If I had looked during that Christmas Eve for people in our overcrowded church filled with an appetite for war or hatred against the British, French, Russians or other peoples – I probably would not have found any. That this Christmas 1941 should be my last Christmas celebration at home until the end of the war, I could not foresee at that time.

The comfortable days at home flew by, and immediately at the beginning of 1942 I was back on the train towards the Luxembourg border and the RAD camp in Irrel.

Here, too, the consequences of war became gradually noticeable, and various reductions and supply shortages arose. Food had not improved. In general it was not bad, but could have always been a little more abundant for us young lads.

Due to the weather, construction work was halted. Besides the customary lessons we exercised in the small hall, cleared much snow, drilled on the parade ground, and learned further songs and how to attach buttons in darning and sewing lessons. After the early morning exercise we still ran bare-chested across the open grounds to the wash rooms, even at minus 20 degrees Celsius. It did not bother us, since our bodies were still heated up from running. Somehow this procedure held a certain appeal for us, for it toughened us up and kept us fit. At any rate, colds or flu did not occur. The clear air and heavy frost made it probably even too cold for the viruses.

Occasionally we were deployed in town or its surroundings when there was the chance to help out extended families, farms and craft enterprises in order to support large-scale projects that could not be done by their own means. We did so with increasing enthusiasm as a diversion; for besides general recognition we most often also received in addition something to eat or drink.

At the end of February, when the days became longer again, we began building new accommodation, and this was accompanied by the usual duties.

At the beginning of March, some weeks before completing our time at the Reich Labour Service, two handsome, tall and blond men of the Waffen-SS [military arm of the SS] in dashing black uniforms appeared one morning. As we were all due for muster for general military service in the near future, as a rule with the Wehrmacht, they canvassed for entry into their organization with enticing offers. According to them, the future belonged to the SS, and who served in it belonged to the elite of the Greater German Reich and the Aryan race. At the end of the presentations they asked who wanted to volunteer for service with the SS. None of us stood up, nobody raised their hand and voice. After general murmuring and whispering suddenly an unpleasant, tense silence prevailed.

The spokesman looked around and pointed at three of us who were tall, blond and athletic and said: 'You will report after the lesson to the camp command headquarters for entry into the Waffen-SS. We will see each other later, until then!'

I felt a stab through the heart. I of all people had been selected and I would have to report with the other two chosen. I was uneasy about this honour. It was not the feeling of fear of something new, but rather an intuitive rejection and the uneasy feeling about joining an organization close to the party, which would have meant furthermore that I would have been stationed even farther from home.

So I decided to ignore the summons and not to go to the gentlemen in black. I hoped that the gentlemen would content themselves with a haul of only two 'voluntary reports'. Indeed they left. I was ordered immediately after to the camp commander. As ordered, I covered the distance to the command headquarters running, and still out of breath I reported smartly to the barracks of camp command.

'Labour Service Man Sauer, why did you not follow the summons of the two gentlemen of the Waffen-SS?' the camp commander asked in a calm and polite tone.

'Because it is my greatest wish to report to the Luftwaffe [air force] after my time at the Reich Labour Service in order to become a fighter pilot. I want to fly a Messerschmitt Bf 109,' I replied promptly.

I surprised myself how smoothly this excuse passed my lips. After all, I knew that the Waffen-SS had no air force of its own. My argument, stated seriously and confidently, had its effect. Subsequently there were still some general questions, and the matter seemed to be resolved for now. This was not the case, but I did not learn this until some months later. The two other comrades had volunteered. I have never learned whether or not they survived the war.

A few days later the rumour went around the camp that we would be dismissed from Reich Labour Service ahead of schedule. For a change this proved to be true, for there were many rumours and watchwords, and as a rule wishful thinking was behind them.

The entire camp was in high spirits, as at the end of March we were indeed released three months earlier than intended to our great joy. Naturally this did not happen without a reason or out of Christian love. No, after the devastating war winter at the Eastern Front and the disastrous losses of the Wehrmacht, the muster stations were operating at full stretch.

The front needed fresh supplies of men and material. The losses of the German Wehrmacht at the Eastern Front alone amounted to roughly one million fallen and missing after just a few months of deployment. Many losses were due to the unimaginably harsh Russian winter, for which the German leadership had not or only wholly insufficiently prepared the soldiers. After all, inside the Führer's headquarters they had assumed that the Red Army could be forced to capitulate after a campaign of just a few weeks.

During the last roll-call the camp commander gave a short speech, which also addressed love for the German people and service to the Fatherland. Following this, we packed our few belongings and said goodbye to the many likeable comrades with whom we had spent time in the Reich Labour Service safe and sound. Just like before Christmas, we travelled the same route home into an even more uncertain future. We parted company and most of our friends and comrades we never saw again.

The time in the RAD camp had not killed or damaged us. We learned such useful things as cleaning, laundry, darning and sewing, were schooled in discipline and punctuality, comradeship, willingness to help and solidarity, learned respect, consideration, attention and self-confidence. As we generally came from families with a fixed Christian world view, the then unavoidable ideological indoctrination had little effect on us.

Boys and girls alike were drafted to the Reich Labour Service between their seventeenth and eighteenth years.

The day before yesterday we had been children and yesterday adolescents. Now we were considered seasoned, grown men overnight who were burdened with the hardships of war without restrictions.

2

Call-Up for the Wehrmacht

Only a few days after my release from the labour service and my safe return home I received a letter in which I was ordered to muster.

I received this letter at a time when our armies in the east were involved in desperate fights. The German leadership had learned nothing from Napoleon's fate and the experience of a two-front war from 1914 to 1918. To attack Russia, moreover with an inadequately equipped army, was an irresponsible, criminal adventure, Russian roulette, but with five bullets instead of one in the revolver drum.

In January 1942, along a front of 600 kilometres, thirty-seven German divisions of Army Group South were faced by ninety-five Russian divisions. By March 1942 the losses of the entire German eastern armies amounted to 1,107,000 men. The Army Group Centre was able to confront the opposing 190 Soviet divisions with only sixty-seven exhausted German divisions along a defensive section of 1,000 kilometres. In the area of Army Group North, thirty-one weakened German divisions fought along a front section of 600 kilometres against eighty-six Russian divisions. On all fronts the Russians outnumbered the Wehrmacht three times to one. Yet we did not know that. We were used to the reports of success on the radio, which had come thick and fast in summer 1941, and were at best wondering why we heard so little of them now. Thus at the scheduled date I travelled on time and in good spirits to the muster in Coblenz.

The enormous number of young recruits on this early morning was overwhelming. The masses were jostling in the corridors and I looked into curious, expectant and euphoric, but sometimes also fearful and sceptical faces. Everywhere there was hectic and busy activity, steered by orders in a loud, clear and unmistakable military command language.

The medical examination took the following form: in a long row personal details were registered. In a room opposite we had to undress completely. As soon as your own name was read out, you had to call loud and clear 'Yes, sir!'

in order to subsequently enter a large examination room. This proceeded in a jiffy, as the respondents were not examined one by one, as earlier in Irrel, but in groups of eight by three doctors just as thorough as they were fast. The medical personnel consisted of a senior surgeon major, an assistant doctor with the rank of a senior lieutenant and a junior doctor in lieutenant's uniform as a scribe. In the course of the examination among other things height (1.82m) and weight (78kg) were determined and a blood sample taken in order to define the blood type (I was type O). This was also stamped on the aluminium dog tag. In this way the blood type could be immediately determined in case of injury. If a soldier had fallen, one half of the tag was broke off and taken along.

Then followed the famous so-called 'Please cough' while we stood eight men in a row. For me this procedure was nothing new, but many newcomers were among us: A-level graduates who had taken emergency exams ahead of schedule, or members of the late 1924 school intake who in part no longer had to participate in labour service before being drafted into the military. The reasons were obvious. All front units reported ever-increasing losses and had an insatiable hunger for 'cannon fodder'.

During this examination the assistant doctor gripped the testicles of each of us not too gently in order to detect any scrotal hernia. If the results were positive, the matter was resolved through an operation carried out at short notice in order to render the comrade fit for duty. It did not matter for this examination whether the doctor had cold or warm hands; it was simply an unpleasant sensation, and the new, inexperienced comrades made many an inappropriately comical sound, which was answered by hearty laughter from the others and commented upon by the doctors in smutty squaddie jargon.

There subsequently followed the command 'About face and bend!' – the pinnacle of the embarrassing procedure. The assistant doctor examined each of us between the legs in order to detect haemorrhoids, which of course he almost never found in such young men. Yet what he found with a boy standing next to me, made him laugh out loud: 'Here we have one whom we should send straight to the cavalry. Everything is green. The lad brought his own fodder to the muster.'

Another cackle followed. The boy from Westerwald turned bright red and I felt quite some pity for him. He must have felt an urgent need and then wiped his bum with tufts of grass.

For me the mustering procedure was over at lunchtime. On the spur of the moment I used the opportunity to stroll around the town, and took the time to look in on my old apprentice barbershop of the Stillings family in the Rheinstraße. There was great joy when I visited, especially when they learned that I was stationed in Coblenz and was still safe and sound in these troubled times. Mrs Stillings wished me luck and sent her best regards to my mother.

Although there had been several air raid alarms in Coblenz, the town had so far been spared bombing damage. I therefore experienced it in its original splendid flair with the castle, the festival hall, the theatre and all the magnificent squares, streets and houses in the baroque and art deco style. Only the window displays of the shops were not as abundant as two years ago. There were not the same great number of visitors, either, and the austerity caused by the war was felt everywhere.

Only six days after the muster our postman brought my draft notice for training with the infantry. Immediately afterwards I was intended for deployment to Infantry Regiment No. 437. This regiment was part of the 132nd Infantry Division and was at that time at the Eastern Front with Army Group Centre advancing on the Crimea and the city of Sevastopol. For that purpose I was to report at the given time, 14 April 1942, to the Gneisenau barracks in Coblenz-Horchheim.

So I marched once more with my usual luggage to our train station and took the early train to the main station in Coblenz. From there I took the tram along the upper Löhrstraße to Kaiser-Wilhelm-Ring (today Friedrich-Ebert-Ring) past splendid buildings, among them the festival hall (today Rhine-Moselle-Hall), further to the Pfaffendorf Bridge across the Rhine to its right bank and through Pfaffenheim to Horchheim. At the final station 'Alte Heerstraße [Old Military Road]' I alighted and had to climb up the long mountain slope to the large, modern Augusta and Gneisenau barracks newly built in 1937–38 and close to the Deines-Bruchmüller barracks in Niderlahnstein.

My barracks bore the name of the General Field Marshal Neidhardt von Gneisenau, who in 1805 had defended the town of Kolberg in Western Pomerania at the Baltic Sea against Napoleon and his allies and later contributed in a decisive manner to the success of the wars of liberation as a reformer of the Prussian army. Having reached the guard post of the barracks, I was received by the sergeant of the guard together with numerous other recruits. Everyone received a marching note for the induction.

A quick, uncomplicated ritual followed similar to the procedure that I had got to know in the RAD camp, albeit in an intensified form: company building and the allocation of barrack rooms, receipt of all parts of the uniform and equipment including bed linen and so forth. Everything was conducted on the double without pause by loud and clear commands from the instructors. In contrast to the RAD camp, the entire building complex of the Gneisenau barracks was new, large, spacious and extremely modern.

Kitchen, mess hall, barrack rooms and sanitary installations consisting of toilets and showers were new and of generous proportions. The portions from the team kitchen were sufficient and tasty. Despite the drill and rough tone, I experienced the stay at the barracks as more pleasant than that in the RAD camp. Somehow we felt seasoned in contrast to the newcomers who had been drafted to the military immediately after school and apprenticeship and had not known any ideological indoctrination and paramilitary training apart from the Hitler Youth. Among them were in particular active farmers who were not drafted into Reich Labour Service and A-level graduates, some of whom were already a little older.

The first days and weeks were especially hard and unfamiliar for those comrades. Basic training was no picnic, but after a certain time one got used to the many novelties, exertions and vexations. Apart from a very few exceptions, all could cope with the tight drill after a short while.

In the first two days 250 men were drafted. When I arrived in my room laid out for twelve men on the first floor, I could barely believe my eyes. With his back to me and diligently making up his bed was standing my friend, the butcher's journeyman Paul Seidenfuß.

'Why, Paul, you old horse butcher! I can't believe it! Tell me that I am not hallucinating. How on earth are you in the same room at the same time in the same barracks as me?'

'That cannot be coincidence and certainly is a good omen,' Paul replied and laughed happily, while we embraced each other.

'Now that we are back together after such a short time, absolutely nothing can happen to us during this war.'

Only a few moments later another comrade entered the room and probably witnessed our greeting ceremony. 'I am also called Paul, Paul Severin, and am from Andernach.' This third comrade was almost a head taller than me, an A-level graduate, and as a complete greenhorn he found the first days in the Wehrmacht much more strenuous than us two. We became fast friends with this affable lad. All in all we were lucky with our call-up, as we could fulfil our general military training in our home town Coblenz.

During this we attentively followed the daily propaganda news and front reports. According to them, after the spring offensive in the east the German Wehrmacht was advancing unstoppably against Stalin's Red Army. One Russian army after another had capitulated. Huge areas in the Ukraine were conquered. As a result we did our duty in the hope that the war would soon be won and we would no longer need to go to the front.

Early in the morning at 5am the sergeant of the guard woke us with terrible bellowing, which resounded through the long corridors of our company building. Then followed the usual morning ritual that we already knew: early morning exercise, washing, cleaning of rooms and precinct, breakfast and roll-call at 7am. Then followed lessons in all aspects of the military, drilling on the parade ground, paramedical training, instructions in wearing gas masks, firearms training with carbine 98k, pistol 08 and the new machine gun 42. We were, after all, in the German infantry, the 'queen of all weapons', as it was said in squaddie jargon. I, however, could not comprehend the comparison to a queen, but rather had the impression that we were the poorest sods of the Wehrmacht – and to be honest, we were and it became even more so at the front.

The days were often very long, and we fell into our beds bone tired. We tried to get as much sleep as possible in the few hours available.

Due to the short nights and the constant sleep deficit, some seemed to be mentally affected: we had a terribly slow, fearful and stuttering boy called Jakob in our room, who out of sheer fright at 4 am began, an hour before the wake-up call, to put on his uniform, to make his bed and to get everything ready, just so that he was done in time and would not attract the negative attention of the sergeant of the guard. To the displeasure of us other eleven roommates, he robbed us of an hour of precious sleep. The next days we helped him where we could for the sake of peace and quiet. After the second week the comrade had become fast and self-confident, and all twelve soldiers in our room returned to the usual sleep rhythm.

Jakob could not get rid of his stutter for a long time. It was particularly bad for him on the days when it was his turn to sign off the room to the sergeant of the guard. Out of nervousness he floundered even more when speaking and was barely able to utter one correct sentence. We often could not suppress our laughter and pushed our faces into the linen of our cots. Also, the respective sergeant of the guard did not conceal his derision. That was, of course, bad for Jakob, and thus we all decided to teach the poor lad to speak slowly and calmly. We rehearsed signing off the room with Jakob like on a theatre stage, and in this manner gradually gave him more surety and self-confidence. It worked, and after a short while he had shed his speech impediment. He was mightily proud of his faithful friends and we of him. For clear speech and clear, short commands were not only important in the grounds during firearms training, but also in firefights where they could be lifesaving depending on the situations and enemy fire.

Besides Paul Seidenfuß, Paul Severin and Jakob Schmitz, I would now like to introduce the rest of our room. Two boys were from Bavaria and were called Markus Heinrich and Toni Grad. Klaus Baulig came from my neighbouring village, Mülheim, Georg Bauder from Mannheim, Ulrich Schmidt from Siegen, Herbert Niederländer from Saarbrücken, Robert Kleinz from Rüsselsheim and Heinz Luft from Düsseldorf. The latter very soon turned into a problem for all of us.

Heinz was one of those oddballs whom I had already encountered during labour service, but somehow was entirely different again. He behaved in an even more extreme way, seemed to suffer from a pathological image neurosis and did not fit into our room, into our corridor, into our circle of comrades. His big mouth or his 'Schnüss', as it was called in the Rhineland, was vitriolic, loud and never stood still. Although he was also capable of speaking at room volume level, which could be observed occasionally, he had to constantly act up, make a din and told all kinds of nonsense besides some half-truths. He was a 'blabbermouth before the Lord', always played to the gallery and wanted to draw attention at any cost, but was of no use for anything because of his limited intelligence. He could never restrain himself, constantly looked for a victim whom he could keep on at and got massively on the nerves of everybody in his vicinity with his obtrusive manner.

His piercing voice resounded through all corridors and stairwells. He incessantly sang obscene songs, told primitive, vulgar jokes and otherwise only uttered nonsense. He butted into all conversations without grasping their contents, he could keep nothing to himself, he had to broadcast everything immediately, wherein he wavered between superficial knowledge and pure fairy tale. In the morning he said 'good evening', in the evening 'good morning'. At Easter he met us with 'Merry Christmas' or 'Happy New Year', just as the mood took him.

Based on his bragging and his vocabulary, we suspected that he came from the world of pimps and prostitutes. At any rate this man was stressful and unreliable and made sure that our room drew negative attention time and again. In addition he was very fond of alcohol, and it seemed that his whole interest was focussed on eating and drinking.

During military training in the barracks and grounds he presented an incalculable risk, especially during exercises with weapons. If it was 'To the left' during morning roll-call and all fifty-two men of our platoon followed the command, Heinz turned to the right. With his shenanigans he pushed our nice platoon leader Sergeant Engelbert Haymann, who like our room-mate Klaus Baulig came from my neighbouring village Mülheim – both were incidentally cousins – to the brink of madness.

Haymann bellowed in such cases: 'You singularly stupid fool, you total idiot, left is where the thumb is right,' which just increased the confusion. While marching Heinz warbled away with one of his frivolous songs and knocked the entire troop out of stride. Naturally he was ordered to punishment drill, but even that had no effect. The toughest instructors broke their teeth on this mug.

Usually such a troublemaker would have been certain of a 'visitation from the Holy Ghost', but due to the expected futility of such action we desisted from this kind of pedagogical measure.

One morning during roll-call in front of the rooms in our long corridor, when everybody was standing straight in uniform, Heinz arrived before the sergeants of the guard in pyjamas, looked a proper idiot and trailed a long string behind him. At its end he had tied his toothbrush, spoke with it like with a dog and repeatedly called: 'Come, Fiffi, at heel, Fiffi.' We roared with laughter. Heinz clearly played the 'nutter', but had finally overstepped the mark with this appearance.

When we returned to our room in the evening after duty, Luft's bed and locker had been cleared out. Whether he was committed to the then asylum in Andernach, later called the state mental hospital, or ended up in prison or even a punishment battalion, we never found out. We were just glad that this stupid idiot was finally gone. I personally do not believe that he was mad, rather I considered him a shirker and dissembler. Yet this scam had little prospect of success at that time.

The allocation of barrack rooms was made according to height. Together with my comrades, I was among the tallest in the first room. In the second room the comrades were shorter so that the height of the soldiers decreased proportionally with the higher room numbers. On the second day I became friends with the burly farmer Josef Reif from Dieblich-Berg at the Moselle, who was only 1.67m tall and hence in the last room, as well as with the farmer Paul Wagner from Nörtershausen. Since I came from a farm myself, we had enough things to talk about in our sparse free time. Furthermore, I, as an experienced labour service graduate, had the opportunity to support Josef, Paul and other comrades during the difficult initial phase of basic training in word and deed. This once led to the following operation in which I thoroughly failed, but which fortunately ended in a close shave for all of us. On the first nights the air raid alarm sirens sounded across Coblenz and our barracks. We had orders to go to the basement rooms in this eventuality and to return to our rooms after the all-clear signal. Josef, as an experienced farmer, however, had to go to the horse stables after the all-clear in order to calm down the animals, and if necessary to lead them from the halls and only then to return to his room.

At last, after the fourth night of alarm, and with a permanent sleep deficit, I convinced Josef to simply stay with me in the basement and catch up on sleep there until duty. The previous day I had actually discovered a room with beds that some sergeants and corporals used during the day for 'naps'. What the latter allowed themselves during the day, we tried in the following night ourselves during the alarm. Yet in our case we did not lie atop the cots, but beneath them and slept so deeply after the alarm had ended that we were roughly woken only late in the morning around 10am, when the sun's rays were already shining into the basement room. Our corpulent company sergeant major, Staff Sergeant Groß, had looked for us like for needles in a haystack and finally found us under the beds in the basement. Full of rage he yelled at us:

'You bloody shirkers, are you crazy? We have been looking for you for hours on the entire barrack grounds and you have pissed off to this very basement. I will make you do punishment drills! Detention and curfew for an indeterminable time period will be added, too. We are not in the circus here, where every monkey can do as he pleases!'

It was my luck that during the night I had wrapped a shawl around my neck due to the low temperature. Now I declared with a faked hoarse and barely audible voice: 'I am ill, have pharyngitis, Staff Sergeant sir. Can no longer talk.'

My comrade Josef Reif had no on-the-spot excuse. We both feared a draconian punishment. However, because we had not sworn the oath yet during the first days of training, we got off lightly with a severe rebuke. The main reason for this unexpected clemency was the fact that every man was supposed to take part in taking the oath to Adolf Hitler on 20 April, the 'Führer's' birthday, at the Augusta barracks next door only six days after our enlistment. Only Josef, who had grossly neglected the horses entrusted to him, received a more spectacular than severe punishment by Staff Sergeant Groß. He had to clasp a thick, long wooden club between his legs and to ride past us several times as on a wooden horse while neighing, during which process Groß whipped his bum slightly with a riding crop. The laughter was indescribable and Josef laughed most of all. However, my laughter stuck in my throat, for God knows this incident could have had far worse consequences for us.

For outdoor or firearms training we had to step up at 7am. In full gear, we then marched up the steep incline to 'Schmitten summit', the local military training area. Corporal Kleinschmitt and Corporal Josef Bauer from Miesenheim were in the habit of ordering us to put on our gas masks during the steepest section while singing three songs. What often made the mindless marching more entertaining became torture under the gas mask while climbing the mountain. We had barely air to breathe and the additional singing was difficult for us. Perhaps this procedure was supposed to strengthen our lungs or to prepare us for worse things to come. Yet, since Corporal Kleinschmitt, in contrast to Corporal Bauer, used to order this procedure every time, I played a trick by moving my jaw slightly, taking a deep breath, but not actually singing. After other comrades had imitated me and the volume of the marching column had decreased, Kleinschmitt stepped closer to us to listen. Every time we saw in the corner of our eye that he was approaching, we bawled out the appropriate song with hollow voices from beneath our gas masks, until he moved away again. He could not see us laughing beneath our masks, but that actually cost us even more air. Nevertheless, we enjoyed our laughter, for we had a waggish sense of humour and had not yet forgotten how to laugh.

During the fourth week, a battalion muster took place. At 2pm we stood prim and proper in smartened uniforms on the parade ground. An inspection by our regiment commander, Lieutenant Colonel Kindsmüller, had been announced. At the command from our company sergeant major 'First rank advance five steps, second rank advance three steps' the entire battalion began to move and formed two passages. Kindsmüller walked along the length of the front of all three rows and looked into the face of each and every one of us. He began in the last row, and since due to my height I stood in the first row next to Klaus Baulig and Paul Severin, he only passed us towards the end. Exactly in front of me, he came to a halt and looked intently into my face: 'Your name?'

'Private Sauer, Lieutenant Colonel sir.'

This was followed by another question: 'Would you like to become my batman?'

I answered with a loud: 'Yes sir, Lieutenant Colonel sir!'

'Private Sauer, report to me at the command office after the muster!'

I reported properly, standing to attention, and as ordered went immediately after to Lieutenant Colonel Kindsmüller. This man radiated a confident calmness and impressed me as a kind of caring father figure. He offered me a cigarette straightaway and politely explained in a few sentences my additional tasks. These consisted mainly in polishing shoes and boots, to arrange the uniform properly, fetch food if required as well as running errands, messages and other minor matters. These activities did not release me in any way from my daily duties though, but were deducted from already sparse free time.

He inquired after my age, origin, parents and profession. When I told him of the early death of my father, this man who age-wise could have been my father became very quiet and thoughtful.

'My wife and I recently experienced a very cruel fate, too.' While he spoke, he looked motionless and rigid out of the window. 'Our beloved son has fallen during the spring offensive of our Wehrmacht at the Eastern Front at the age of 19. Our Fritz was a wonderful person and was only one year older than you.'

When I then mentioned that I bore the same first name, an oppressive silence prevailed inside the room, and I felt the sadness of the older man. At that moment I could feel sharply how deeply affected he was by the death of his son. Only later at the front I realised that Lieutenant Colonel Kindsmüller viewed me as a kind of surrogate son and that I had found in him a surrogate father.

In the following week some competitions were held in our battalion to determine the best athletes. These took place not only at our Gneisenau barracks, but in all other barracks and military institutions of the wider surroundings. Almost 20,000 soldiers were stationed in Coblenz town and district at that time. The reason for the selection of athletes was that the regional capital Coblenz planned and minutely organized a great athletics festival in Oberwerth stadium a fortnight later. Since my athletic achievements had already been recognised, besides the general barrack duties and my duties as a batman for our commander I received two hours off every day to complete the appropriate training for this event. Yet I only had the opportunity to train together with some other select comrades after dinner at 6pm.

Here I was, of course, in my element again and looked forward to the evenings, regardless of how tedious and difficult duty had been during the day. I was, after all, a passionate sportsman. Even early on I was always among the best. Some interesting occurrences sprang to my mind once more in this context. Our youth did, of course, not only consist of work or of us teasing other people by boyish pranks. Unpleasant people whom we could not stand, who had already drawn our attention in a negative way and who had annoyed or beaten us justly or unjustly became, nevertheless, the occasional victims of our pranks. Yet these were rather harmless, and we never broke or destroyed anything. If, however, a door or gate handle was smeared with wagon grease, for example, many a nominee appeared late for Sunday Mass with a black hand. We then looked closely to see if our prank had worked on our chosen victim.

Yet if Father learned of such shenanigans, the prank was paid for with a severe scolding or a few smacks to the bottom. Most of the time he did not catch me though, since I could run faster than him. I still can recall two such situations clearly. Firstly, it came to light that I, together with my best friends Edgar Weiber and Arnold Lohner, had tied a tin can to the tail of an ugly, incessantly barking, stupid stray village dog, as a result of which the poor dog had raced yowling along Altengärtenweg towards Bur, while the can rattled behind him on the pavement.

'I am truly sorry and it will never happen again,' I called to Father when I came home.

The local village gossip mill had already betrayed us, and Father ran after me into the barn carrying a stick. Breathless, he came to a halt at the bottom of the ladder, while I climbed as high as possible into the straw, almost reaching the roof of the barn. Hunger drove me down again after an hour and into the kitchen. Luckily Father had gone to the Lindenhof around the corner for half a pint of wine, and thus the precarious affair became quickly forgotten with the help of Mother's mediation.

Another time some of us boys were caught smoking in secret and received detention and punitive tasks at school. Somehow Father learned of this before I came home from school. When, upon my return, I recognised his shoes behind our yard gate I knew immediately that the writing was on the wall.

Only flight forward remained. I opened the gate and ran past my baffled father into the kitchen. He immediately came after me, and when he found me in the kitchen doing a headstand with my bottom to the wall, the situation was defused, as Father had to laugh heartily. His Fritzje got off lightly again with a new trick. Somehow I sensed that Father was secretly very proud of my imagination, my quickness and my athletic abilities.

My boyish courage was sufficient for secretly smoking with my classmates, but it quickly left me when once a year the mobile dentist arrived at school with his car full of horrible instruments, as had happened every year since 1933. All school children including the teachers had to undergo a preventive dental examination. In fear of this ceremony, I regularly vanished and ran home to Mother. Yet she brought me back to school, and I could no longer escape the nice dentist with his mechanical dental drill. That we received some sweets as a reward afterwards did not help us avoid the need for treatment, and in the following year I made my next attempt to escape. Unfortunately I was among those students who never evaded the drill.

In my youth I was not only shaped by my parents, but also by the then still rather strict Catholic church. Not only every Sunday and every holiday, but also on numerous other occasions, we had to go to mass. This, of course, took up a considerable amount of our precious spare time. Raised as a good Christian, I naturally believed in God, and I have never forgotten how to pray, especially later during the war in Russia and up until old age. Nevertheless, I did not feel like accepting the offer of our parish priest to be appointed altar boy.

For our caring father it was naturally a matter of course that his children went to mass regularly and decently dressed every Sunday. Therefore he could be found every Sunday morning in our laundry room next to the barn, polishing the high hobnailed shoes for us four boys and hammering the occasional missing nail into the leather soles.

I, on the other hand, preferred to spend my spare time on our sports grounds next to the brook. I was drawn there every free minute, and early on I recognised that sport was my greatest passion. Here I could vent my need for movement. We played handball every day and occasionally football, as far as the weather permitted it. Here the exciting games of our first team in field handball took place. The TV Bassenheim 1911 e.V. played in the Rhineland first league, at the time the top league in the German Reich. The starting whistle was always blown at 2pm on a Sunday. If the strong teams of Green-White Mendig, Welling, Weibern, Mülheim, Kärlich or Urmitz competed, our village was deserted and everybody was standing around the playing field. Sometimes, during top-class fixtures, there were almost 2,000 people in the crowd, including those who had travelled mainly on foot or hitched a ride on open trucks.

For my first Holy Communion on Low Sunday in 1932 my parents gave me a real leather handball. At that time this was my most treasured possession. Now there were no limits to daily training any more, and I was more than happy.

Besides handball, athletics such as throwing, running and jumping were my favourite. For instance, I often frequented the old long jump pit, whose contents consisted only of a thin layer of sand that furthermore was enriched by stones or sometimes dog excrement. I trained throwing with everything I got my hands on, from gravel stone to a spear made from hazel wood I had carved myself.

For weeks in advance I looked forward excitedly to the annual sports competitions and intensified my training. When the great day arrived, the tension was enormous. In sixth to eighth grade I received the highest number of points, and the prize was at least a laurel wreath. I recall clearly that I threw the 80g leather balls almost from one goal to the opposite one. However, the sports ground was not 100 metres long as usual, but only 90 metres. Nevertheless it was quite far.

During long jump I often heard some people shout: 'Fritz is jumping! Fritz is jumping!' And thus more than two dozen spectators were often gathered around the long jump pit cheering me on. As a result of my frequent training of jump shots in handball – being right-handed – my left leg had developed a high jumping power. I always achieved lengths well above six metres in the three attempts to jump for every participant from the seventh grade onwards. Without special training and in view of the heavy and poor-quality sport shoes as well as the inadequate runway this was a remarkable achievement.

In field handball I had several role models in the first team from whom I learned much in terms of technique and tricks by watching. I played in the youth teams in the centre half position due to my speed. One has to know that a team in the then popular large field handball consisted of eleven players as in football. Besides the goalkeeper, four players formed the defence and were only allowed to be in their own half of the playing field. Four players were in the offence and had to stay in the opposition's half. The two centre halves, in contrast, could play in both defence and offence. These two players thus had to cope with a lot of running over the full distance. Besides reinforcing the defence and offence, their principal task was to intercept the ball and to pass it on as quickly as possible to their own offence, before the two opposite centre halves could positions themselves in the defence. Some older spectators called me the 'deer', probably due to my sprinting ability and jumping power. To be honest, I was very proud of this.

Two of my role models in sports I wish to mention here. There was on the one hand the outstanding goalkeeper Paul Theisen, who would fall during the war, and on the other hand Josef Ringel of the school cohort of 1914. He survived the war and later had a textile and grocery shop in Mayener Street. Josef was in the squad of the 1936 German Field Handball Olympic Team in Berlin, and that was something very special to us. He had the nickname 'I'. Simply 'I' like India. The reason was that during a jump shot with the release of the ball he very loudly exhaled in order to give the ball a high release velocity. Hereby he made a sound like 'Ihhhhhhhhjehhhh', and so his nickname was born.

I was especially fascinated then by the film about the 1936 Olympics made using the most modern means by Leni Riefenstahl. Since I had seen it for the first time in the newsreel at the cinema, I had dreamed of the opportunity to participate as a decathlete in a future Olympic Games. Perhaps 1944, I thought, or 1948 or 1952. I could not have known that it would be sixteen years before a German team was again allowed to participate in the Olympic Games again – 1952 in Helsinki. My thoughts were constantly revolving around sports then. Whenever and wherever I found the opportunity I trained in all kinds of disciplines, mainly throwing, running and jumping. I even took part in the training of the successful Bassenheim wrestling team, which due to the lack of a sports hall took place in the two function rooms of the village public houses Korn and Poll, and learned many a trick there.

On the day of the sports festival we marched with our delegation down the Old Military Road, crossed over the Horchheim railway bridge to the other bank of the Rhine, and via this route reached the sports facilities immediately. The Oberwerth stadium became filled with a large number of athletes and spectators. I estimate the number of active sportsmen at significantly more than 300. Although small delegations from all sports clubs in the vicinity were present, the overwhelming number of competitors consisted of soldiers, labour service members and Hitler Youth. How were the sports clubs supposed to set up large teams, since the suitable members had now been fighting for almost three years at the fronts?

I was registered for the multi-event, and so I fully enjoyed the free day. Physically and mentally absolutely fit, I could match my achievements in running, jumping and throwing as planned. In the late afternoon the victory ceremony took place, and I was endlessly proud that I had achieved the highest number of points in the multi-event. For the victory ceremony I had to climb onto a pedestal and a laurel wreath was placed upon my head. In addition I received a scrapbook with stickers of all the then customary trades and furthermore an additional day of special leave.

My dreams of participating in the Olympic Games were fuelled by this success, but the political and military events of the following years meant that these remained dreams. The next day, after a commendation by the commander the daily military drill was ever-present again. The training period came to a close as new soldiers were needed at the Eastern Front. The barracks were needed for the next generation of recruits.

During the last week a parade of our troops took place at the confluence of Rhine and Moselle, the modern-day Deutsches Eck (German Corner). This was a huge evening spectacle with marching music played by a large military band of the Wehrmacht. To the strains of the 'Rider's March of the Grand Elector', we marched in six rows past the monument for Emperor Wilhelm I and continued in goose step to the sounds of the 'Badenweiler March' and the 'Yorck March'. During this ceremony we felt part of a great national community and felt strong, powerful and invincible – an impression that was soon to change.

Apart from this impressive ceremony, my enthusiasm for the military was limited though. I could not acquire a great taste for warcraft and especially for the general two-year conscription, which later was extended indefinitely due to the unending war. Training had turned us into dashing and outstandingly honed soldiers, but to go to war was not on our personal agenda, and this was true for all of my closest comrades. Yet we had no other option – not in this war and not in this political system.

During one of the last mornings with lessons in the auditorium of our barracks we learned that Cologne had been reduced to rubble on 31 May 1942 during the first raid of the Royal Air Force to use 1,000 bombers. Only ruins remained of the beautiful historic town and thousands of residential buildings towered over by the soot-blackened Gothic cathedral. This first large-scale raid had mainly targeted the civilian population; industrial installations were hardly affected. There were thousands of dead women, children and old people. We were very shocked and expressed our sympathy to our Cologne comrade Jakob Schmitz. His worried expression only brightened again after several days, when he learned that his family's house had been destroyed by bombs, but they had survived the attack unscathed in a bunker.

The day after next, shortly before our transfer to the military training area at Baumholder, we were vaccinated in the medical area of our barracks against all kinds of diseases that could threaten us at the front, as for example typhoid, tetanus and so on. It was a short, quick stepping up. The recruits were standing with bare upper torsos in a row reaching well outside the main entrance of the building, and the vaccinations were administered as if on a conveyor belt.

Only two metres in front of me stood the gigantic Paul Severin. Over the shoulders of the men in front of us we saw our staff surgeon handling an enormous syringe. With this he jabbed quickly and professionally one recruit after another into their chest – always with the same needle, mind you. The closer we came to our vaccination, the whiter Paul's face became. When the doctor pressed the needle of the large syringe into the chest of the last man in front of him, Paul suddenly rolled up his eyes in a funny way, gasped for air and weaved his arms about. I just was able to call: 'Paul, where do you think you're going?', but the tall lad was already lying unconscious at the feet of the baffled staff surgeon. Paul still received all the vaccinations, too, but as the last man in our battalion, after he had recovered from his fear of syringes.

3

To the Eastern Front and the 132nd Infantry Division

It was only a short distance from Coblenz through the picturesque Rhine valley with the Loreley rock and all the splendid castles until Bingerbrück and further through the Nahe valley until I reached Baumholder in the Western Palatinate and the large military training area there.

I had used the one day of additional leave granted to me to visit home once more three days before our troop transfer. There I settled some important matters and with a heavy heart said goodbye to Mother, my brothers Hans and Karl as well as to relatives and friends.

In one compartment with my closest comrades I travelled by train for four hours including stopover time to the new residence of our battalion. While the romantic landscape of the Rhine valley passed us by, most of us either were in their thoughts at home or brooded over the dangers most likely expecting us.

On the huge military training area we were once more accommodated in barracks like those in the Reich Labour Service. Our room sharing constellation remained almost completely the same and was complemented with four new comrades. They were all nice, and soon we were a tight-knit team again.

Klaus Baulig, our bureaucrat of the communal administration Weißenthurm, reported to the Luftwaffe, where he was allocated to a bomber squadron of Heinkel He 111 bombers. Also Sergeant Engelbert Haymann, our friendly platoon leader with the warm heart and exemplary leadership qualities, had left us. The tall and muscular man who in civilian life was a blacksmith volunteered for the 'Greater Germany' Division at the front. We were all very sad about that. Only a few years older than us, he had almost become like a father to us with his cordial, honest manner.

Daily duty focussed on field, combat and firearms training, whereby formal duty receded into the background. Whoever achieved more than ninety rings during target practice with ten shots from the carbine 98k to the ten-ring target was not only allowed to march back to the barracks earlier that afternoon, but was off duty after firearm cleaning, too. We exploited this little freedom several times thanks to our good shooting technique. We had already learned shooting rather well before our military training. At our Bassenheim fair on the former village green (today Walpot Square) there was a shooting gallery that invited you to shoot and to spend money with a pithy catchphrase from imperial times: 'Train eye and hand for the Fatherland!' There we shot with air rifles, not to train for war, but to win a cheap artificial flower, a picture postcard or similar prizes.

In Baumholder our preparation for the impending deployment to the front took place. The Wehrmacht was an offensive army. The storm attack at the command 'Take the high ground' and under shouts of 'Hooray' was trained daily. In contrast, defensive tactics were a foreign word for the trainers. Later we would bitterly regret this deficiency and during the costly rear-guard actions at the collapsing Eastern Front we had to learn these tactics fast in order to survive. Yet at that time we were still secretly hoping for an imminent end of the war, as it was promised us in the continuing reports of success of the Wehrmacht on the radio and in the vigorous speeches of Minister for Propaganda Goebbels. When it then became known that we were to complete training after the fourth week and to be deployed to the Eastern Front by train, our mood was anything but thrilled.

Shortly before our departure our parents and relatives had the opportunity to say goodbye to us in our camp at Baumholder. We were not allowed to go home. I informed my mother of this in a short letter. In answer she visited me, together with Aunt Anna, her sister-in-law, just like numerous other mothers, fathers and wives. For many it became a farewell forever.

The two elderly ladies had never before travelled beyond Mayen and Coblenz, and the train journey was an adventure for them. And yet in modern terms Baumholder in the Western Palatinate was not far. We were able to chat for two hours. Mother reported on the house and farm, on my brothers and on local events. A French and a Polish prisoner of war would help on our farm, as was also common for other farmers in the village. They would live in our house and would also share the family meals.

I was particularly pleased with the large food parcel from Mother, but this joy was dampened by the worry about the future.

After a short, heartfelt goodbye, the two women commenced their arduous journey back on crowded trains.

Our journey into the unknown began a few days later. After the troop transport train had been loaded with weapons, ammunition and food, we boarded the wagons on 5 July 1942 with half of our battalion. Another train followed the next day with the remainder of our unit. I was lucky to travel on the first train as the commander's batman – in a second-class compartment occupied by many of our officers and sergeants. The railway transport started around noon and first went via Frankfurt/Main East Station. During our short stop we had the opportunity to shop for our personal needs. From there we continued via Fulda, Dresden, Wroclaw, Cracow, Lviv, Kiev, Kharkov and Odessa towards the front on the Crimea peninsula. It was a beautiful summer, and in peacetime we could have enjoyed the journey, but horror awaited us.

From the second-class compartment I could admire enchanting landscapes, lakes, forests, fields, villages, castles and forts, cloisters and towns with splendid buildings. Germany seemed to me to have sprung from a romantic book of fairy tales. Nothing indicated that it was in the middle of a murderous war. In horrible contrast to this idyll stood the destruction that our troops had brought about during their advance towards the east and which we would see for ourselves a few days later. Just now we could take pleasure in the view of all these beauties one last time, since we did not foresee what was waiting for us.

I cannot deny that during these hours I was proud of our country. The first verse of our national anthem sprang into my mind, 'Germany, Germany above all, above all in the world'. The song written by Hoffmann von Fallersleben in 1841, which later became our national anthem, originated at the time of German regionalism, decades before national unification. The aggressive nationalist meaning with which it was imbued during the world wars would have been alien to the poet. I also understood the text rather as an affirmation of the value of one's home. After all, we left behind a country still intact to the largest extent in which order, punctuality, regularity and cleanliness prevailed. On the other hand, we thought incessantly about what would probably be waiting for us in this strange country thousands of kilometres away, against which we fought a war of previously unknown cruelty. Not that we were afraid. We believed ourselves to be well prepared and through National Socialist propaganda highly motivated and certain of victory. Amidst so many faithful comrades and led by officers, sergeants and corporals worthy of trust, we considered ourselves to be relatively secure as soldiers of a highly modern, outstandingly trained army.

On the third day of our monotonous journey towards the front interrupted by numerous stopovers, we could sense the endless expanses of a huge country. Never in my life I had been so far away from home. The journey went towards the south-east and led deeper and deeper into the Ukraine and towards Russia. We did not need to take into account the time difference related to this. In Germany, as in all occupied territories, German summer time applied. This measure did not only save energy, especially important during times of war, but also facilitated communications between the military high command and the units scattered across the whole of Europe.

On this third day of our journey my commander, Lieutenant Colonel Kindsmüller, spoke to me about the sense or rather the lunacy of this war and about his concerns regarding its future course. He had already told me, when all others in our compartment were standing outside in the corridor to smoke and our private conversation was concealed by the monotonous clattering of the train's wheels:

> Fritz, this damned war against the huge Russia cannot be won by tiny Germany, although we call ourselves now the Greater German Reich and our crazy leader unduly taxes our abilities, does not accept our inferiority in personnel and material, but believes he can offset it through soldierly courage as well as the tactical and technical superiority of our Wehrmacht and Luftwaffe. The front is pulled further and further apart and now stretches from Leningrad in the north to the Crimea peninsula on the Black Sea in the south. This is far more than 3,000 kilometres. We need more and more soldiers, the transport routes for supplies become farther and farther. The losses in material and especially in fallen and wounded men are immense. In addition we waste our forces in other countries, especially in the Balkans and in North Africa, just because this megalomaniac Mussolini wishes to resurrect the old Roman Empire and in the process catches one defeat after another. I do not wish to burden your heart, my boy, but I am of the firm

opinion that the matter will not end well. Do not tell this to anybody, otherwise we will both be hanged or shot.

He further advised me to be alert as soon as we would reach the front and I should take good care of myself. How desperate must this fine staff officer have been that he unburdened his heart to me, his batman and a simple soldier? Finally he told me in confidence:

> In the RAD camp in Irrel a negative remark was written in your file due to your rejection of voluntary entry into the Waffen-SS, of which you most likely have not known anything until today. I have removed and obliterated that remark.

I was touched and speechless about the trust he placed in me. 'Many heartfelt thanks, Lieutenant Colonel Sir,' were the only words I managed to utter. His enlightening, moving words I have never forgotten, and for the first time I began to doubt that I would see my home ever again.

At the end of this relatively comfortable journey, after one week on the train and with many hours of waiting at various stations, especially in Kiev and Kharkov, we reached the Crimea peninsula. Our direct delivery to the 133nd Infantry Division then began.

Due to the continuing rapid advance of the Army Group South we were unloaded quite a distance from our marching destination, the town Feodosia on the Black Sea. Runways, bridges and railway tracks were under construction by the Todt Organization and our pioneer units, but could not keep up with the fast progress of the German units. Therefore we marched in tremendous day marches towards our unit. During the breaks I looked for support, security and optimism in my closest comrades: Herbert Niederländer, Markus Heinrich, Toni Grad, Robert Kleinz, Ulrich Schmidt and Georg Bauder. We only spoke the absolute necessary. Nobody probably wanted to comment upon the gloomy mood and the uncomfortable feeling. The temperatures in the south of Russia were exceedingly high, and after a short while we suffered quite considerably from thirst. Daily we had to make between 40 and 50 kilometres with our field kits. Since we were not a fully motorised unit, the few vehicles we had were needed for the transport of fuel, ammunition and food supplies. We could only inhale their dust and the stench of diesel. Actually, only twenty of the 220 German divisions deployed during the Second World War were fully motorised. All other units had, of course, their own vehicle pool, but this was cobbled together from captured vehicles and other cars. Otherwise the Wehrmacht depended on the railway, millions of horses and, just like old times, on the boots of its soldiers.

During our few rest periods I was continually overwhelmed by a great tiredness in the searing heat so that within a minute or two I fell into a deep sleep in the trench next to the road. Every time I impressed upon several comrades to wake me up before setting off again, and luckily I could depend on them.

On the road we marched through typical Russian villages that were partly still standing, but most of the time they were more or less strongly affected by the preceding hostilities. Time and again I could observe that women, children and older men met us with cordial friendliness, frank pleasure and without mistrust, although we were already in the second year of our war with the Soviet Union. They waved at us in a friendly manner, partly received us with flowers and most of all gave us fresh water from their wells and cisterns. I encountered amiable, helpful and cordial Ukrainian and Russian people with whom we could have struck up friendships – if only the damned, god-forbidden war had not been!

The indigenous population apparently still viewed us as liberators from Stalin's yoke. After all, countless people – estimates speak of up to 20 million casualties – had fallen victim to his innumerable cleanses, had perished in the gulags or had been tortured and shot in the basements of the NKVD, and the Ukraine had suffered in particular during the persecution of the kulaks [peasants wealthy enough to own a farm and hire labour], which had been directed against the more affluent rural population.

Only later did we also learn that our own security services, police and SS commands, allegedly in part also supported by Wehrmacht units, had carried off and murdered people, especially those of Jewish faith. To this were added the reprisals against partisans who committed attacks on German soldiers. Furthermore, blond children were deported to Germany and there were placed in homes or with foster parents without children of their own.

A population to all appearances initially liberated from Communism, whether in the Ukraine, Belarus or in the Baltic states – Estonia, Latvia and Lithuania – soon enough was subjected to the next terror regime in form of the occupier's administration and the murderous action groups. Trapped in the National Socialist racial mania, the chance was gambled away to win over the people. On the basis of numerous personal conversations I was able to have with native people there in the course of the next days, weeks and months, I gathered the impression that many volunteers would have gone into battle with us against Stalin given appropriate treatment.

During the hours of marching in the oppressive heat through the south of Russia we cursed all those to whom we owed this misery. At night we simply lay down on the ground in the open air next to the dusty roads and went to sleep. During the monotonous marching in columns we could muse on the sense or nonsense of this lunatic enterprise. Not much was spoken, and we very soon lost the appetite for singing soldiers' songs. Too heavy was the burden of kit, carbine 98k, ammunition, gas mask, belt support braces, steel helmet, haversack, food, water flask, side arm and uniform parts. Amidst the column we were alone with our thoughts.

Of course, we thought of home every day. Yet one time, I can still recall it clearly, I thought about what kind of people I would consider role models as an eighteen-year-old. No politicians sprang to mind, least of all our 'Führer' Adolf Hitler, the fat Reich Marshal Hermann Göring or the nagging, nasty little runt Josef Goebbels. The leading representatives of the NSDAP were particularly disliked by me and most of my comrades. As young as we were, we still felt instinctively that these demagogues brought calamity over us and our homeland. Yet they were in charge at that time and led our country, our people and our youth, and together with us numerous other nations, into a catastrophe of thus far unknown dimensions. Among the representatives of the party, at best the Reich Youth leader Baldur von Schirach seemed to us humane, moderate and perhaps even likeable. He was especially popular with the teenagers from the Hitler Youth and the League of German Girls.

Our role models came rather from the world of sports such as the boxing world champion Max Schmeling or the racing driver Bernd Rosemeyer, who had a fatal accident during his attempt to break the speed world record with his Auto Union racing car. We also worshipped creative artists such as Leni Riefenstahl, who inspired us with her films, or the aviation pioneer Elly Beinhorn, who flew once around the world in her Klemm KL 26. Among the singers Zarah Leander, Lale Andersen and Hans Albers were popular, among the film actors the comedians Heinz Rühmann, Theo Lingen and Hans Moser, and also Heinrich George and Willy Fritsch. During the war particularly successful soldiers were, of course, turned into role models, too, among them the flying aces Mölders, Galland, Wick and Marseille, the 'star of Africa'. Apart from Galland, all of them fell. Hans-Joachim Marseille crashed after 158 air victories as a young captain in the North African desert when he was only twenty-three years old. To these were added some generals who were successful and tested in the eyes of soldiers such as General Field Marshal Rommel, the 'desert fox', Colonel General Heinz Guderian and General Field Marshal Erich von Manstein.

Perhaps the persons named were rather idols than true role models, since they were employed by the Nazi propaganda in order to strengthen our fighting spirit. Yet after the first deployment at the Russian front at the latest they lost their importance in view of the cruel reality of war.

Until then, however, we were in good spirits. Together with me, 400 men, or rather mere chits of boys and adolescents, were marching towards the east. We were all thoroughly fit, athletic, slim, of rude health and convinced that we fulfilled our duty for a just cause. None of us could imagine that most of us would be ill, wounded or had fallen after a few days, weeks and months. Only a lucky few managed to survive their front deployment unaffected over a longer period of time.

In mid-July 1942 we finally reached our destination, the town Feodosia, and to my wonderment I saw the Black Sea for the first time in my life. Here we learned that the Crimea peninsula had been almost completely conquered by the German Wehrmacht only a few days previously and that only minor skirmishes were still fought in a few sections. This news delighted us all the more, since we were quite exhausted after the long journey by train and the following marches on foot.

The 132nd Infantry Division was set up on 5 October 1940 in Landshut, Bavaria, Military District VII, as a division of the eleventh wave of new military formations. The personnel was provided in equal parts from the 263rd and the 268th Infantry Divisions. The structure of the division consisted of the three infantry regiments, 436, 437 and 438, the artillery regiment 132, the pioneer battalion 132, the anti-tank battalion 132, the intelligence battalion 132 and supply troops. It had a normal strength of 15,000 men in total. The first war deployment of the 132nd Infantry Division took place during the Balkans campaign. In June 1941 it took part in the attack on the Soviet Union in the context of Operation *Barbarossa*. With the Army Group South it marched from Lviv via Ostrog and Shitomir until Kiev.

In November 1941 it operated on the Crimea and belonged to the attack units that were supposed to conquer Sevastopol. Together with the 54th Army Corps, it attacked the port city from the northern direction and the mountain slopes of Belbek Valley but met fierce resistance, which became set in the defensive belts around the city. In December 1941 fighting was concentrated around Kamyshly Gorge and the Summit 192. Storm battalions and pioneer battalions of the 132nd Infantry Division gained only six kilometres of ground during the first days of combat.

From January 1942 General Fritz Lindemann took over the division leadership on site. On 30 March the division was now assessed as suitable only for limited offensive tasks. At this time an average infantry company had only a combat or trench strength of sixty to seventy men, thus at maximum roughly a third of the required strength.

On 7 May 1942 the division began an offensive with artillery attacks and the landing of assault craft against the 44th Soviet Army east of Feodosia at the heavily fortified isthmus of Prymorskyi. In June 1942 the final attack on Sevastopol was undertaken. Hereby the 132nd Infantry Division together with the 54th Army Corps formed the focal point.

As the 132nd Infantry Division had lost roughly a third of its personnel, the division now had to be removed completely from the front only a few days before the conquest of Crimea by the 54th Army Corps due to the loss of a further 3,167 men in the battle for Sevastopol. In total the German and Romanian units lost around 35,500 men during the eight-month battle.

In Feodosia and its surroundings all the troop parts of the melted down 132nd Infantry Division were therefore scheduled for replenishment and were waiting for urgently required reinforcements. This included our battalion among others.

After our first restless and hot night in Feodosia the situation briefing followed in the early morning after reveille and a hasty breakfast. I prepared myself for my general duty and additionally for the service to my regiment commander – a task that continued for me.

4

The Journey into Uncertainty

We were quickly integrated into the units allocated to us and enjoyed the time of replenishment during the hot Russian summer. General military duty was reduced to the bare necessities in view of the heat, and so I had more time again to care for the well-being of our regiment commander, who in the meantime had been promoted to colonel. Yet the duties asked were restricted to polishing boots, keeping the uniform in order, fetching meals and post and other trivial assistance, and thus I was able to furnish many of my comrades with a short haircut appropriate for the season. For my numerous customers this service was, of course, free of charge, although I gladly accepted any cigarettes slipped to me.

I could satisfy my athletic ambitions in our time off duty with runs along the Black Sea beach – an absurdity amidst a horrific war increasing in bitterness and cruelty, during which countless soldiers died day in and day out along the thousands of kilometres of the front. This recovery phase in a subtropic climate was on the one hand a welcome diversion for us. On the other hand we looked greatly worried into the uncertain future of this operation. It seemed as if the war wanted to take a short breather before devouring us. While others bled out, I, the eighteen-year-old private Fritz Sauer from the little village Bassenheim in Vordereifel, was on holiday at the Black Sea. My comrades and I could barely grasp our short-lived luck during a deceptive calm, and we enjoyed the gorgeous days as much as it was possible and our time off duty allowed.

I was good at a variety of sports, but I had never had the opportunity to learn swimming as a child. Therefore, at the first opportunity I cautiously ventured into the pleasantly warm water of the Black Sea dressed only in my underpants. Due to the high salt content and the resulting strong buoyancy, I learned how to swim in a matter of hours. At every opportunity presenting itself to me I was lying in the waters of the Black Sea and enthusiastically practised crawl, breast and backstroke. For a short time I deemed myself to be in paradise and yet soon enough found myself in hell.

Fortunately the losses due to illness were sparse in our battalion – in contrast to the division. Daily men reported sick due to rampant dysentery and due to the lack of drinking water, which was torturous in the great heat. It was so bad that almost daily numerous men not only fell ill, but an increasing number died. Older squaddies advised us to eat onions, which were very abundant here. I ate these fat onions like apples, as many as I could find. Fortunately I was spared the dysentery, whereby it never has become clear if and how much this was due to the onion diet.

During this rather contemplative short breather for our unit a horrible incident occurred: one soldier of the 132nd Infantry Division had raped a Russian girl serving as a voluntary assistant for the Wehrmacht. He had been convicted of the deed twice, and in such cases military justice knew no mercy. Within hours the man stood in front of a court martial, was sentenced to death and hanged. This spread like wildfire around the entire division and had the effect that none of us hit on the idea of laying our hands on a Russian girl.

After a few weeks of replenishment, the division was facing its next combat mission. Together with other units freed up after the conquest of the Crimea, it was integrated into the 6th Army under the command of Colonel General Friedrich Paulus. This army was intended to conquer that city at the Volga River that bore Stalin's name – one of the most ill-fated orders of the 'Bohemian private' who called himself Führer. If this measure had remained in place, it is probable that none of us would have seen home again. Yet a little later the 132nd Infantry Division was assigned to the 11th Army and transferred to Army Group North. There it was supposed to be deployed in a specific section of the Ladoga and Volkhov front in the Leningrad area, but ended up some time later under the command of the 18th Army. Of all of this we knew nothing at the beginning of our transport by train. Our commander was constantly travelling to the division staff due to various situation briefings. I did not see him for days, for which reason I could not obtain any more detailed information.

In the period from 28 August to 10 September 1942 the entire division was sent from Kerch, Feodosia and Simferopol on several freight trains. Our battalion was entrained on 1 September in Simferopol. Instead of the endless marches there was at least some tight space on a freight carriage. Together with my closest comrades, I was jammed into a carriage in such manner that we could just about sit on the floor. We went, with several interruptions, via Kherson, Nikolayev, Berdichev, Rovno, Kovel, Brest, Bialystok, Elk and further towards Insterburg.

The rumour mill was grinding at high speed. On every occasion, for example when taking on food supplies or bunkering water and coal for the steam locomotive, one unfounded rumour chased the next. When we reached East Prussian soil we were all in good spirits. For while reading the German place names on the boards of the cute train stations it almost seemed as if we had escaped the war for a short while. Or perhaps even forever? Was the war possibly over for us before it had even really started? Stirred up by the varying prophecies of our wise guys, most of us actually believed that the war would not last much longer and that we would all soon go home again. From Insterburg to Königsberg it was a mere puddle jump.

This happy expectation should soon turn out to be fatal self-deception. Yet for now we did not suspect anything and were all in the highest spirits despite the tiring transport by train, which affected us relatively little.

The 52-class locomotive pulled our overly long and fully laden troop transport train with moderate speed through a lovely, slightly hilly landscape. At the beginning of September 1942 East Prussia showed itself from its most beautiful side. Passing by, we experienced a country so beautiful as I had hardly ever encountered so far. Countless large, dark lakes and forests interchanged with well-kept farms and estates whose fields and lands were almost unimaginably large, a unique paradise of nature rich in animals, especially in big game, fish and horses. I observed this splendid land through the wagon door pushed wide open with astonished eyes and enjoyed the contrast with the ugly images of death, chaos, suffering and destruction only experienced on our march through Russia.

We continued to travel at low speed through numerous faraway places of East Prussia, and once again I was seized by a sense of pride in our beautiful homeland formed by many generations of industrious people. At the same time I was overcome by the first serious doubts about our political leadership, who had jeopardised all this in an insane war instead of preserving it carefully. I began to understand my parents, who rejected Hitler's regime, although they restrained themselves from loud criticism in fear of reprisals.

The propaganda washing over us day by day gave the impression that the Allies had been driven into a war of destruction against Germany by the Jews. Yet if this war was actually only the defence against an unjustified attack from outside – why then was the Wehrmacht fighting across all of Europe, and in addition in North Africa? And why did they try to persuade us that we were a 'people without space', when East Prussia's expanses alone could have taken in a multiple of population? These questions occupied us during the long hours of idleness, but, of course, we did not dare to utter them aloud. We knew after all how 'defeatists' and 'subverters of the war effort' were treated.

The fact was that at that time the world was ruled by a lust for power, megalomania and cynical political calculations – at the cost of the youth of all nations at war. Whether nationalism, imperialism or Communism, all abused us for the reckless safeguarding of the various power interests. We were made into henchmen of death and destruction in the belief we were fighting for a just cause, especially against Communism. I also sensed this critical attitude against the political and military leadership in my comrades during the endless talks while the carriage slowly rattled along. We were all too keen to travel home immediately to our parents, families, friends and our everyday life and to pursue our actual professions. Yet this wish remained unfilled for us for a long time, for many of us forever.

Our train stood for more than four hours on side tracks at Insterburg station. We all received a plentiful, hearty warm meal and could top up our water supplies. Meanwhile, hectic activities by the accompanying officers and non-commissioned officers unfolded. Commands echoed throughout the train. Large quantities of provisions and rations were loaded and an additional carriage added, probably with ammunition. The coal car was stacked anew and the water kettles of the locomotive filled. Several trains passed our train after a short stop. An ambulance train laden to the full with wounded soldiers heading for Berlin was dispatched the fastest. A large number of Red Cross nurses caused a dramatic flurry of activity, when they loudly demanded provisions and bandages. I watched as some soldiers who had apparently died during transport were carried from the wagons, and this sight was anything but motivation to us.

After this longish stopover the locomotive started to move again, whizzing and hissing, and drove towards the north. We reached Tilsit, crossed the Neman (Memel) River and drove through the former Memel Territory, which as a result of the Versailles Treaty had been split off from Germany but had since been reconquered.

Where the German railway network ended and the Russian broad track network began, we were transferred to a waiting train, and the journey continued through the Baltic states. Lithuania, Latvia and Estonia had been annexed in 1940 by the Soviet Union as a consequence of the German–Soviet Non-Aggression Pact, but after the Wehrmacht's offensive on Russia occupied by the latter. This short spell under Communist rule had sufficed to antagonise the non-Russian population so much towards Stalinism that thousands of Balts reported for duty with the Wehrmacht, but most of all with the 15th, 19th or 20th Grenadier Division of the Waffen-SS. In contrast, the population of Russian origin fought for the most part on the side of the Red Army against German occupation.

Slowly and monotonously we rolled through a largely flat landscape. While slowly passing a construction site, we could observe at least forty prisoners working in the area of the railway tracks. We could not discern whether they were criminals, prisoners of war or Jews. I felt pity for the people, but none of us knew why everything was the way it was. None of us could have changed or prevented it, nobody could have liberated the people, stopped our train and redirected it home. No, we were sitting on a troop transport train that after passing the construction site drove full steam ahead north towards an uncertain destination and even more uncertain fate.

When we rolled farther and farther north through the Baltic states past the towns of Šiauliai, Jelgava, Riga, Valga and Pskov, every wise guy knew which hour the bell had tolled. Since Insterburg we had been travelling straight to a new front, new dangers and possibly towards death. The mood dropped to the floor, and fearful silence accompanied us for the rest of our journey. Driving through the Russian towns of Luga, Lissina and later below Leningrad and the already closed encirclement around the city through units of our Army Group North, we reached the town Mga not far from the besieged city.

5

No Hope of Return

Having reached the train station at Mga, completely overcrowded with far more than a thousand soldiers, we had reached the stop closest to the front that could be reached by train. A troop transport train that had arrived shortly before us was standing on neighbouring tracks. A desolate backwater at the end of the world, were my first thoughts despite the busy activities. While my comrades and I were overwhelmed by an increasing unease, the first commands resounded, and officers and sergeants shouted their orders along the two trains. In the shortest time all the carriages were cleared of people and materiel. We were informed that we were relatively close to the front and had to reckon at any time with aerial attacks by Russian bombers and fighter pilots.

Within half a day's march we reached the section of front intended for us and the positions, trench systems, shelters and provisional bunkers consisting of thick timbers laid on top of each other with a soil cover, all of them erected by our predecessors.

We relieved a bled out and battle-weary infantry unit in the Gaitolovo area, who had been waiting longingly for us for days and had held out bravely. The sight of these men left no doubt what we were facing. They were emaciated and the deprivations of the recent weeks were not only visible in their uniforms and appearance, but especially in their posture and facial expressions. These were no proud and dashing parade ground soldiers any more. Here the clocks were ticking differently. And this theatre of operations had also nothing in common with the warm south of Russia and the beaches of the Black Sea. Here, far to the north, we found ourselves at the 'arse-end of the world', if you will forgive me this vulgar expression of squaddie slang.

What on earth were we looking for here in this endless wasteland more than 2,300 kilometres away from our beautiful homeland? Nothing, nothing at all! We all were completely at the wrong spot in this country. However, we could not change the current situation, and whining helped us little. As

so often during this time, we had to arrange ourselves with the given circumstances as well as we could. Our strong bond of comradeship helped to
overcome depression, homesickness and fear. After only a few days we all had
lice due to the lack of hygiene and we could not get rid of them.

The thunder of our own artillery was now to be heard at a close distance.
The 105mm pieces fired constant harassing fire in a monotonous sequence.
The induction into our positions and accommodation was carried out in a
prompt fashion according to squads, platoons and companies. We now found
ourselves with the 132nd Infantry Division in the orbit of the 11th and 18th
Armies in the middle of the front of Army Group North.

When we learned late in the morning that early morning the next day we
were supposed to go into our attack position, our mood dropped to the bottom. At lunch a copious amount of good kettle goulash made out of horse
meat was dished out, but I barely managed to eat one bite. The advice of the
experienced, older squaddies would not leave my mind, according to which
it was better to attack on an empty stomach because the survival chances
in the event of sustaining a stomach wound would increase – provided the
injury was limited, extrication in time was possible and short-notice medical
treatment ensured.

So the afternoon passed and also the evening with bleak thoughts con-
cerning the impending mission, and it was not a precaution due to a potential
stomach shot that made my evening ration literally stick in my throat.

In the morning at 3:30am we were woken and made ready for the assault.
Corporal Kleinschmidt appeared in our sparse shelter and distributed several bottles of hard liquor, one each for four men. Upon my question as to
why this was a good idea he answered me that a little alcohol would soothe
the nerves and dampen the fear. As until then I had hardly ever drunk strong
alcohol, I gave this courage booster a miss like many other comrades.

At dawn our first attack followed after half an hour of artillery fire at the
Russian positions. With 'Jump, march, march!' and loud hoorays we jumped
out from our cover simultaneously with several hundred comrades and
stormed towards the enemy, firing wildly.

We received relatively little fire and managed to make larger gains in territory in the shortest of time. Our then still strong artillery had done good
work with their precise shooting and considerably weakened the enemy's first
line. Yet still during our rapid advance we suddenly received strong mortar

fire from the rear Russian lines. From all sides we heard 'Take cover!' and shouted orders to dig in.

Further progress under this fire was out of the question, so our assault stalled and came to a halt. As far as it was possible, everybody looked for a ditch or a shell crater, or started to dig himself in with the collapsible spade carried by everyone. I sought cover in a depression of perhaps 30 centimetres and pressed myself as deep as possible into the churned up soil that smelled of gun powder. Body and legs were stretched out and spread, including the toes, in order to present as little a target for firing and spray effect as possible – just as we had practised countless times up on the Schmittenhöhe and in Baumholder in the course of our training. To the left of me were Markus, Herbert and Uli. Out of the corner of my eye I saw to my right a comrade from the neighbouring platoon lying down in cover just like me eight to ten metres away. During the inferno of the battle noise I was constantly muttering to myself: 'God, help me, do not let me die, God, help me, do not let me die.'

The mortar shells struck untargeted, but damned close, sometimes in front, sometimes at the back of us. The air was filled with dirt, dust, stones and acrid gun smoke. We heard splinters and projectiles buzzing loudly above us in the dawn. It is a miserable feeling to lie helpless amidst battery fire, not to be able to do anything and to have to wait for further orders.

In the meantime our artillery observers had picked out most of the Russian mortar positions and took them under precise fire. During this crossfire a Russian mortar shell struck between the spread legs of the comrade lying under cover to the right of me and exploded around the height of his knees. My blood froze. Some seconds after the explosion the boy shouted like crazy 'my legs, my legs' and I watched as he rubbed his lacerated and partly torn off leg stumps with both of his hands in a half sitting, half lying position. Blood pumped out of the stumps in a pulsating manner. The screams were like those of an animal. They seemed to me to last an eternity.

I had the sensation of having to pee or shit into my trousers, but there was nothing for me to expel, since I had not eaten anything since yesterday lunch due to the sheer tension. At that moment I regretted that I had not drunk any of the damned liquor – preferably half a bottle by myself – in order to have to bear this horror around me only in a drunken stupor and to be able to forget these terrible images. I was entirely sober, however, wide awake and full of adrenalin.

It took about eight to ten minutes until the comrade next to me fell silent. Presumably he had bled out. It was horrible: these screams, this battle noise, the flashes of mortars and burst of projectiles. Where had we got ourselves? What had they done with us? The drudgeries in the Reich Labour Service and at the Gneisenau barracks seemed almost like paradise at this moment of utter despair. Why oh why had our path led us into this hell?

The artillery duel of our cannons against the grenade launchers of the Soviets was quickly decided. Our offensive was continued, and early mid-morning the set goal was achieved. All my former barrack room comrades and friends had remained unharmed, thank God.

The following day the next offensive was ordered. Our devoted corporal Kleinschmidt appeared the evening before for a situation briefing in our makeshift shelter erected in the afternoon. This time he dragged along an old rucksack with two thick cured sausages, a fresh loaf of army bread from the division bakery and two bottles of vodka, which he had scavenged for our group from our company master sergeant, Sergeant Major Groß, the so-called mother of the company. With great appetite we all ate of the tasty sausage and the fresh bread without thinking about the possibility of an injury during the next mission, since we had just survived the first hot deployment safe and sound. During the night, however, the terrible images of the dying boy caught up with me again and robbed me of the little sleep remaining until dawn.

After reveille most of my comrades barely managed to eat a bite due to the tension. It was the same for me. Before preparing for the assault I tried the vodka and, remembering the previous day, I quickly drank two large gulps. Never before had I drunk such strong stuff, and it took my breath away. I struggled for air and vomited most of it out again. As a consequence I started this second attack absolutely sober again and with a clear mind. Getting drunk was avoided by our entire group in future, while the Red Army soldiers virtually had a skinful of vodka.

We stormed forward under the covering fire of our MG 42, the old carbine 98k in the crook of our arms and two stick grenades at our belts. We were not undaunted by death, did not have the intention to die a hero's death. No, wholly on the contrary! To survive and to return home was our top priority. Before this and all following missions we all endured mortal fear, and we gave each other encouragements. One was there for the other, even if the situation was as dangerous as can be. Care, consideration and an unbelievably reliable comradeship helped us to bear the horror. From this tried and tested community we gained the optimism and hope for survival. Here and now the harsh training of the Wehrmacht paid off, too.

Our squad also survived the second attack unharmed, although the platoon and company had to chalk up some losses. Then, after a day's pause, the same procedure followed, and the whole affair was repeated in a similar manner.

Almost daily we infantrymen were confronted with death, and the gruesome sight of corpses and terribly disfigured bodies discomforted all of us severely.

It must have been my fifth or sixth assault, when amidst the enemy fire a heavy thunderstorm came down. After days of heat the atmosphere was so charged that the thunder rumbled as incessantly as the pieces of the Russian artillery. Completely soaked, I threw myself down into the dirt three metres from a mighty tree together with Ulrich Schmidt, looking for the next available cover. We deemed ourselves to be safe for a short while, when with a terrible crack a lightning bolt struck just this tree. The tree went up in flames immediately and was ablaze. Nothing had happened to us, but we jumped up in fear for our lives and looked for another hole in which to take cover.

We also survived this day unharmed, although dying was omnipresent around us. When we came more or less to rest late in the evening next to our comrades in the tightness of the positions, we never knew if we would see the next morning, and I prayed to God whenever I could to protect me and save me from death. We were all just so young and our entire lives with all their dreams were actually still ahead of us. Even more dangerous were the days. Would a new offensive be ordered? Or did we have to reckon with a Russian counter-attack? The incessant, fierce battles were intense and full of losses.

We stayed fixed in the same place before Leningrad at the beginning of September 1942 in the most northern section of Army Group North under the leadership of General Field Marshal Wilhelm Ritter von Leeb and later in the formation of the 18th Army under Colonel General von Küchler, although the German offensive of the Army Group South still continued to make good progress. While the situation in the areas of the Army Groups Centre and North remained unchanged to the largest extent, the 6th Army, 250,000 men strong in twenty-two divisions, advanced relentlessly deep into the Russian steppe towards Stalingrad. Despite the scant gains in territory by the Army Groups Centre and North, the German war machine still ran smoothly. At any rate, our units arrived just in time to intercept the Russian counter-offensives.

The logistic effort for the supply of more than three million soldiers in the endless Russian expanse was without parallel. Food, ammunition, bandages, vehicles, equipment, weapons and much more were scant according to the circumstances, but still sufficiently available. As yet the supply operated smoothly – in spite of the enormous distances and the increasing partisan activities in the hinterland. Yet the personnel expenditure was huge. To every front soldier were added nine to ten soldiers in the rear echelon who ensured supplies and provisions.

Even the field postal service was working without a hitch. After a few days we received parcels and letters from home. These were sent to the units at the front with Prussian punctuality.

In our front section I met Colonel Kindsmüller again. I tried once more to do justice to both my duties as far as possible. I only stayed in his vicinity for a short moment each time, but on every occasion he slipped me cigarettes. Smoking dampened my constant hunger and calmed my nerves.

Only two weeks after we had taken up our positions and extended them into a labyrinth of trenches, foxholes and earth bunkers, we were expecting the first large-scale assault on our positions by the Russians after extended artillery fire. They probably wanted to test the fighting strength of the 132nd Infantry Division, new to this section of the front, and stormed towards us with inconceivable masses of men.

We were waiting under safe cover and saw with horror what was approaching us from afar. It was dreadful! The entire horizon, as far as eye could see, was black with people. There must be thousands being thrown into battle. A large part of the soldiers carried no weapons and were driven with pistols by the following political commissars into our defensive fire. If a Russian fell who carried a rifle, one of the unarmed men picked it up and continued storming forward. That a soldier was sent into battle without a weapon was actually inconceivable in the Wehrmacht. Only in the so-called probation units, also called punishment battalions, did such a thing allegedly happen.

When the attacking masses were in firing range, our defensive fire let loose from all weapons upon command. With our old-fashioned but high-quality and precise 98k carbines and only six bullets we could never have stopped these masses. That we could defend ourselves successfully was owed to the modern new MG 42 machine guns. They were relatively light, easy to handle and had an extremely high cadence of 1,500 shots per minute. However, the weapon also used an enormous amount of ammunition, which had to be provided by the MG shooters II and III or had to be dragged to it during battle. It was to our great advantage that overheated barrels could be changed within a few seconds with asbestos gloves.

Our defences included a number of the MG 42s and the Russian assault collapsed under their crossfire. The few survivors flooded in panic back into their initial positions; left behind were countless dead and many screaming wounded who slowly bled out. It was cruel to have to watch, and even worse to listen to, this spectacle. We observed the events in abject terror. On our side some comrades had fallen or been wounded, but all my friends remained unharmed: Markus, Toni, Walter, Robert, Georg, Uli, Herbert – we were all still together.

These attacks were repeated in the course of the next few days again and again in a similar manner with varying intensity. Sometimes there was more artillery fire, sometimes more attacking infantry. If the opportunity offered itself to us to advance under sufficient cover into our manoeuvring area, we extricated shouting or screaming Red Army soldiers, provided first aid to them and brought these poor bastards to our field dressing station for initial treatment. During these quite dangerous explorations we would often observe that a corpse would at first lay on its back and then later on its belly – a sign that others always examined the pockets of the dead for something useful, especially food and cigarettes.

We felt pity for all these fallen young men, whether Russians or our own comrades. We did not harbour any hatred for the enemy, and always the thought was there that these young men, too, all had mothers, fathers and families who would never see their fallen family members again. Here war showed its hideous face, and we would have liked nothing better than to take back these terrible events. The soldier rarely encountered his hero's death on the battlefield in the form of a painless heart or head shot. The rule was instead a horrendous carnage and murder by mutilation, tearing of limbs and laceration of bodies. The cloying stench of death of the many unrecovered corpses constantly befouled the air and became unbearable when the wind blew from the east.

Our own losses had increased considerably in the meantime, but were still manageable in their magnitude. Yet the Russians became stronger and stronger, and most of all more and more.

At the beginning of the third week of our mission a piece of shrapnel tore off Paul Severin's arm. Shortly after, Jakob Schmitz received a shot in the lungs. After quick field recovery and good medical treatment both could be saved. Paul and Jakob were transported back home on an ambulance train. For both of them the war was over, but at what cost?

In the fourth week Robert was lying watch in the foremost ditch with me. He was very restless and stared time and again out of our trench across the raised protective earth wall towards the enemy positions. I said to him several times: 'Just stay put down here under cover. If the Ivan (as we called our Russian adversaries) attacks, we will notice and learn this early enough.'

Yet Robert ignored my warnings. Suddenly I heard a dull impact. When he had lifted his head once more above the protective wall, a shot had hit him full frontal in the forehead through the steel helmet. The Russian sniper had done a perfect job. Robert was killed immediately. I was paralysed from shock. Desperation, anger, grief and helplessness threatened to overcome me, but I was not even allowed to shout or cry loudly.

I pulled the long alarm string reaching to the backward positions. It ended in a tin filled with a few stones, which now clattered loudly. In this way I could inform my comrades in case of immediate danger. Then I shut Robert's eyes, which had seemed to stare at me in astonishment from his blood-smeared face. I waited huddled next to his corpse, until Markus, Walter, Toni and Ulrich, led by Corporal Kleinschmidt, arrived at my position. The few minutes seemed to me like an hour. We carried the corpse back and buried him behind our lines in a soldier's cemetery that had filled up frighteningly fast in the meantime. A simple wooden cross of birch adorned his last resting place next to countless other graves. During the later advance of the Red Army it was vandalised or flattened. Robert, like me, was only eighteen years old.

Day by day not only the mood, but also the weather became worse. The temperature dropped and the rain, mud and sludge increased. Attacks by Russian planes in the neighbouring section caused chaos and commotion. From under my cover I could observe how the Russian aircraft pelted our positions with machine gun fire during several approaches. Yet suddenly a swarm of German Messerschmitt Bf 109 fighter planes appeared, which attacked the Russian fighters and shot them down by the dozen. These were certainly inexperienced Russian pilots who were not familiar with their aircraft yet. We noticed that they carried white stars on the wings, not the usual red. It turned out that these were not Russian, but American types of aircraft, and the Soviets had not repainted them.

We learned later that the United States had been delivering weapons and material to the Allies since 1940, long before Hitler in his megalomania had declared war on the USA on 11 December 1941. From summer 1942 onward huge arms deliveries worth 12 billion dollars were made to the Soviet Union, on the one hand in large convoys across the North Atlantic to the Russian northern port of Murmansk, and on the other hand via Tehran and Persia in the south. In the context of the Lend-Lease Law, the USA and the UK sent 21,000 armoured vehicles and almost 18,000 planes, and in addition a multitude of non-armoured vehicles.

In the continuous fight for daily survival and without the prospect of a turn in our favour, our faith in the political and military leadership vanished and with it our hope for a good end to this entire enterprise. In contrast, my belief in God was growing day by day, night by night. Prayers accompanied me in the silent minutes and strengthened my hope of surviving this apocalypse.

In our dreams we tried to blend out the real observed horror, as far as this was still possible at all in view of the terrible reality. We thought of our beautiful homeland and especially of our nearest and dearest at home. The certainty that our families and a large part of the home population stood firmly behind us soldiers despite the manifold deprivations and the constant threat of bombing raids kept us upright. In dreams we lived through our short youth once more and through our frugal, but carefree, happy and joyous childhood. I often thought of Mother and my brothers Hans, Peter and Karl, and tried to imagine where they were right now and how they were faring at that moment.

And since the provided rations never sufficed to still our hunger, we constantly dreamed of food and any kind of delicacies. At the same time we were content if we had the good fortune to receive an adequate warm meal once a day.

The days became colder and colder, and darkness fell earlier and earlier. It was not long until the first snowflakes announced the coming of winter. We put on whatever clothes we possessed in order to protect ourselves to some extent from the torturous cold, especially during the nights. The lice felt even more comfortable; they were busy biting us, and the itching and scratching found no end. All the tips and tricks of the older squaddies did not help. There was hardly any thought any more of washing, body care, brushing our teeth or general hygiene, at least not regularly and in an adequate manner. Our shelters, partly destroyed by the constant attacks, could not be improved quickly. As a consequence only inadequate accommodation was available to the mass of our soldiers.

My duties as batman for Colonel Kindsmüller were restricted to a minimum. It was too dangerous to run between the trenches and bunkers without cover. In order not to have to sleep in the open in the now prevailing icy cold, we dug numerous foxholes, which also offered some more protection against the constant artillery fire.

I shared a foxhole of 1.80-metre depth with Herbert Niederländer, across which we stretched a thin tent cover at night for protection against the cold. We still froze like hell. I wore everything available to me on my body: a vest, my personal thick flannel shirt, a thick grey woollen jumper, the uniform jacket and the long, but not particularly warm winter coat. To these were added two pairs of long johns, a pair of knitted socks and the not very warm leather boots. Fortunately I still had a pair of extra socks apart from the footwraps. The footwraps were simply wrapped around the feet before slipping into the uncomfortable boots, which had hardened from the moisture. The clothes issued by the Wehrmacht were unsuitable for this weather, and the announced deliveries of new winter clothing did not reach most of the fighting German units in time. To this was added the food situation, wholly inadequate due to the constant enemy activities such as artillery fire, strafers, raiding parties and frontal assaults. During this 'foxhole phase' a warm meal reached us at the foremost front only once or twice a week. I recall very clearly how we were sitting one day in our foxhole knee-deep in water and had to endure six hours of Russian barrage. In this abysmal situation we constantly thought of suffering a direct hit, and so we silently prayed hundreds of Lord's Prayers during these hours of suffering.

It was a desolate existence for weeks during this wartime winter, filled with waiting, enduring, hunger, deprivations, battles and death. Nevertheless, we did not think of surrender. Now experienced at the front, careful and alert, we all wanted to see our homeland again and return to our homes. This bound us together and gave us hope and support. Our great and close comradeship grew in the ever worsening conditions.

Each of us had in the meantime secretly pocketed one of the Soviet passes, as they were dropped above our positions by Russian planes. These guaranteed every German soldier who defected to the Russian troops good treatment with adequate rations. This operation had barely any success, though, for there were only a few deserters in our 132nd Infantry Division, and in my circle of comrades nobody would have got the idea in his head to forsake his friends and simply run off to the enemy. Such behaviour did not meet our ideas of honour and loyalty, and no threats of the death penalty or counter-propaganda were needed to keep us in line. This did not mean, however, that we settled for this life in hell. We all hoped for a quick end to the war and a happy return home – but under the given circumstances there was no prospect of my comrades and me having our wishes fulfilled.

6

My Best Friend

At the beginning of October I received my second letter from my mother. I was chuffed to bits that my name was called out for once during the distribution of the mail by our master sergeant, Sergeant Major Groß. My first mail from home had reached me even in Feodosia at the Black Sea. From my last letter, which I had sent home shortly after our arrival in Mga, Mother knew about my current approximate whereabouts. Because she neither owned a map nor an atlas where she could have looked up the region where I was, she was very worried about my health. Russia was far away for the simple people in the countryside and unimaginably huge. And whoever could read between the lines of the daily propaganda reports had a sense of foreboding. Week by week new rumours made the round through our village. The report of losses in Bassenheim and its surrounding villages became more frequent. Every death note was discussed, and with each one faith in a good ending to the war was diminished.

In July 1942 our immediate neighbour from house number 2, Georg Schnack, had fallen at the age of 33. This was particularly sad since his little son Dieter was only four years old at the time and later could hardly remember his father.

Mother recounted succinctly and factually the usual news from our neighbourhood in her letter to me. I learned that our Hans had been drafted at short notice to an 88mm anti-aircraft cannon unit and was somewhere in France. He had been transferred from a field artillery unit to Brittany and assigned to the gun crew of a heavy coastal battery.

That our oldest brother Hans had been drafted after all struck me as peculiar, since he led an enterprise that was categorised as important to the war effort in the form of our potato wholesale trade and had actually been deferred from military service. Now my youngest brother Karl tended the farm alone together with a French and a Polish prisoner of war. In the meantime, numerous prisoners of war were now allocated to work on farms or in other important enterprises in the villages. For the most part they were integrated into families and sharing their meals at the same table.

Although the letters from home generally did not contain any good news, I still read them countless times. They were some comfort, a link to the homeland, and they let us believe that we were not forgotten.

The following day a strong eastern wind blew the sounds of engines from the Russian side to us, and this increased in the course of the day. According to the dull clang, these could only be tank engines, and many of them. This bode ill. In the early evening our suspicions were confirmed by a report by the forward deployed artillery observer.

We were not equipped in any manner to fight tank attacks, since besides our usual infantry weapons including the MG 42 we only had two 37mm anti-tank cannons, which were derided as 'army door knockers' due to their modest penetrating power. Against the new Russian T-34 tanks they could only have any effect with direct hits in the tread area.

On the eve of the expected attack a brief instruction from division command went to the unit leaders on the foremost line: 'A Russian large-scale attack supported by a great number of accompanying tanks is to be expected in the early hours of the morning of the coming day. If tanks break through, let your own positions be overrun and fight and destroy the enemy tanks from cover with concentrated loads infantry-style.'

There were no soothing reports. We dug ourselves still deeper into our positions, created concentrated loads by bundling multiple stick grenades together and faced the next day fearfully.

At dawn the Russian artillery smothered our positions with numerous salvoes. Our own artillery answered from afar with harassing fire so that the enemy fire was fortunately very imprecise and apart from a few mortars was either too short or too far.

After roughly twenty minutes the cannons abruptly fell silent. A sudden, oppressive silence was cast over our trenches. Yet this only lasted for a short moment, as we heard from afar the dully droning engine sound of the Russian tanks. After a few minutes the sight that presented itself to me and my comrades Markus and Herbert, who were lying next to me, made our blood run cold. At least twelve T-34 tanks with accompanying infantry rolled directly towards our positions and those of the neighbouring sections. The tanks became more and more, and the first salvoes of their cannons came frighteningly close to our positions. In the end I counted more than twenty-five tanks. Our two 37mm anti-tank cannons returned fire, but as expected without much effect.

Thanks to the disciplined leadership in our most forward trenches by Lieutenant Königsfeld and Corporal Kleinschmidt, no panic attacks occurred among the soldiers in spite of the serious situation. At this distance our carbines and machine guns could not yet be deployed for fighting the rapidly advancing infantry, and thus the few minutes of waiting became an unbearable test of our nerves. I could only silently pray: 'Dear God, help me, dear God, do not let me die.'

In viewing the almost thirty T-34 tanks with a huge number of accompanying infantry, our fate seemed sealed. We continued to wait under cover, while the distance became ever shorter. It was a horrible sensation to imagine being overrun and squashed by the tank treads without being able to do anything about it. A terrible, paralysing fear of death overcame us.

Suddenly, the concentrated fire of large-calibre cannons started up not too far away. The battle noise grew louder, and what we saw resembled a practised shooting exercise.

Under direct fire from two directions, the Russian tanks rolling forward were shot down one after another as if in a display. In the additional fire of our infantry weapons the Russian attack collapsed completely after a short while. A sigh of relief travelled through our lines, and our losses were luckily scant.

Yet what had happened? Afterwards we learned that division command had one battery each of four 88mm cannons take positions on both flanks of our defensive section in order to repel the expected enemy attack. These eight cannons were standing in well-camouflaged positions and had not been discovered by enemy intelligence. Thus they were able to bring into action their outstanding penetrating power from not too great a distance and in a direct line of fire. In the end all the tanks were destroyed, unfit to drive or were burning. I could not see a single tank get away undamaged. Countless Red Army soldiers who had fallen, mutilated, wounded and burnt beyond all recognition, were lying in the manoeuvring area. Once again the hideous face of this accursed war stared right at us and brought to mind the fate that was waiting for many of us.

Due to luck and the initiative of our commanders we had survived once again. Yet the horror only receded slowly from our minds. How long would we remain lucky? Time and again the question arose: How long would we survive under these circumstances?

A few days later a similar attack followed, this time with fewer tanks, but with double the strength of infantry. A breaking of the lines in our defensive section was prevented at the last moment because comrades from a Waffen-SS unit came to our assistance. Without their fearless effort all of us in the most forward line would probably have been lost. In the left sections towards the neighbouring division the Russians managed a larger breakthrough, however, which could only be rectified by the self-sacrificing commitment of the SS units and the Wehrmacht soldiers defending there. The losses on both sides were immense.

Shortly before noon, after we had recovered some of our dead comrades, Lieutenant Engelmann appeared in the foremost trench with us. He had chosen Herbert Niederländer and me for a special mission.

'Men, attention! After the early morning artillery fire and the partial breakthrough of the Russians at our lines the telecommunication lines are interrupted. Direct communication of our units with each other is currently not possible. You must bring these documents urgently to the regiment's command post. Return immediately after!'

With these words Engelmann handed us a large sealed envelope and explained to us the position of the command post with the aid of a hand-drawn map.

'Understood, Lieutenant Sir, it will be executed instantly,' we confirmed obligingly, as we both were not unhappy with this mission, since it removed us from the most forward line for some time. We went on our way immediately. We jogged, carbines in our right hands, through several sparse, not always connected copses in a swampy area, crossed several small brooks that had frozen over and reached our goal one hour later. There we handed the documents with a salute as per regulation over to a senior lieutenant unknown to us. We were dismissed without further instructions, and just like that we were on our way back.

We moved quickly, facilitated by the terrain, partly in a slow jog. The region that we had just left gave us the creeps. Partisan activities in the backward front sections were the order of the day. It must have been halfway back, when we were shot at twice from the right front in one of those copses. In any case we heard two loud gun shots, one immediately after the other.

I caught a glimpse of figures running way, when a loud scream by Herbert frightened me to the core. Herbert immediately fell to his knees, bent over and pressed his hands to his belly.

Moaning and pale with fear he stammered: 'Fritz, I am hit, Fritz, my belly, ouch my belly, ouuuch my belly.'

I immediately threw myself down for cover and took care of Herbert on my knees, heedless of the fact that other snipers were possibly lying in wait for us. I turned my brave Herbert on his back and tried to determine where and how seriously he was hit.

'Fritz, it hurts so much. Quickly, look what it is, help me Fritz, please help me,' these words were pressed through Herbert's lips in panic, and he clung to my hands with his whole body shaking.

What on earth was the good chap wearing in this only moderately cold weather? It took a perceived eternity until I had unbuttoned his long coat and the uniform jacket beneath.

'Ouch, ouch, Fritz, oh dear Fritz, it is certainly bad. I am afraid, Fritz, please help me, it hurts so much!'

The sight of the two blood-soaked flannel shirts under the uniform jacket gave me a terrible shock. I pushed the shirts including the vest cautiously up to the chest and discovered with horror a large bullet hole on the right side of Herbert's belly in the region of the liver.

'Is it bad, Fritz? Say something! I want to go home! I want to go home, Fritz! I want to be with my parents. You will help me, Fritz, won't you?' Herbert stammered. Cold sweat was glistening on his forehead.

It was horrible. What was I able to accomplish here all by myself? With my and Herbert's small bandage kit I could not staunch the heavy bleeding. The good paramedical training during our basic training in Coblenz was useless in this situation. Too far away from the next German unit, we were cut off from any medical treatment here. Calling and shouting for help was equally futile. We would have only betrayed our location to the partisans. I at any rate assumed that they were partisans who had been lying in wait for us. After not meeting any problems on the outbound journey we had probably lacked the necessary caution on our way back.

I tried to help up Herbert and to carry him.

'Ouuuch, ouuuch, I can't,' Herbert screamed in pain and pulled his legs up to his belly.

'Fritz, I have to go to the toilet, help me,' he stammered, 'otherwise I will pee in my pants.' He was obviously embarrassed.

I helped him to relieve himself. In that process I sensed due to his distorted facial expression and his ever paler skin that we would not make it, that I would not be able to save him. In one of the most desolate places on this earth I held the moaning Herbert, my good friend, firmly in my arms.

'Herbert, dear Herbert, be calm, soon we try carrying again,' I attempted to soothe him.

Tears of anger and desperation were running over my face. Everything around us seemed so unreal and at the same time so horribly definitive.

'Herbert, you have to hang on. Let me carry you! Come, let me carry you and bring you back,' I implored him, while I cursed this damned war for the umpteenth time.

'I must go home, Fritz, I want to come home again to my parents,' he stammered quietly. In the following hour, which seemed to me like an eternity, nothing more passed his pale lips but weak, moaning and unintelligible sounds. Herbert, my best friend, bled out internally and died in my arms.

For weeks we were had been sharing our lot, told each other everything, dreamed the same dreams of home, of music, of dancing, of girls and of peace. We were always there for each other as good comrades. And now I held in my arms his lifeless, warm body, which only just now had still been breathing. A desperate feeling of impotence rose inside me. He was just eighteen years old like me and would have still had his entire life in front of him. Oh yes, at this moment I hated them all who had driven the youth of so many people into this insane war.

I very carefully laid Herbert on his back and closed his staring eyes, broke off his dog tag and covered him with his long coat. I hung his carbine across my back, loaded my own carbine, cocked it and cautiously crept back to my unit.

In the bunker-like shelter of Lieutenant Engelmann, with a ceiling reinforced by thick round timbers, I breathlessly made my report.

'Mission accomplished, Lieutenant Sir! But we were shot at on the way back, and Private Niederländer has fallen. He received a fatal stomach shot and is lying half an hour from here in a small birch copse. I can lead you there, Lieutenant Sir.'

Without asking who had shot at us he immediately gathered a combat patrol.

'Volunteers forward', Engelmann shouted into a bordering trench outside. 'We must recover Comrade Niederländer.'

All six participants reported immediately as volunteers to bring back Herbert. Hereby it was wholly uncertain if we had been shot at by partisans or an infiltrating Russian raiding party. Corporal Kleinschmidt accompanied us and as a precaution slung a machine gun over his shoulder.

With the greatest caution I led my comrades to the spot where I had left Herbert. After we had searched the terrain in vain for any trace of the snipers, we recovered our dead comrade and carried him back on a stretcher we had taken along.

I could not help with digging his grave. My nerves gave in after I became aware of what had happened. I smoked half a pack of Overstolz cigarettes and just managed to make it in time to the burial ceremony. Some grandiloquent but little comforting words were spoken, and at the end a salute was fired from eight carbines. A simple birch cross marked the grave. That was all.

How little value has one human life, I thought to myself. We were all closer to death than life. Only now I actually became aware that in all likelihood the second shot had been meant for me and that the marksman had probably only missed his target by an inch. Markus Heinrich, who from now on became my faithful and steadfast companion in my protective foxhole, tried to soothe me, but he failed.

7

My Dream Shatters

The approaching winter made the temperature drop during some nights, which were already minus two degrees. We were miserably cold and in these low temperatures we found only a few hours of sleep, if we slept at all. Our regiment had already had several losses due to frostbite. Fingers, hands, feet and toes were in especially serious danger. Our gloves, socks or footwraps and our leather boots were absolutely unsuitable for these temperatures. This frequently led to the amputation of fingers and toes, sometimes even beyond that of hands and feet.

Meanwhile, both sides, we as well as the Russians, began to get settled for the looming winter in the area of the front. Offensive actions decreased considerably. Apart from a few enemy reconnaissance patrols and half-hearted feigned attacks, the next few days remained relatively calm. In the longer lulls in the fighting we had, after a long time, the opportunity for body care once again.

If we had been virtually harassed in our German barracks regarding order and cleanliness through regulations and checks, all these things no longer played a role at the front. Yet despite the lack of opportunities to take care of our bodies, our troops were still not unkempt or even shabby in any way. Within the breathing spaces we had in this desolate existence from time to time, we could wash ourselves in a makeshift manner, brush our teeth, clip our finger and toenails and cut our hair. With scissors organized from somewhere and my comb – which as a hairdresser I carried with me everywhere – I gave many comrades a decent haircut and on request a clean shave, too.

We also had enough time to write letters. In lonely nights with little enemy activities we spoke a lot about home and dreamed ourselves back there.

'Gosh, Markus, what would I give now for a decent potato dish or even better potato dumplings with a large piece of Rhenish marinated pot roast and red cabbage.'

'Your cravings are not bad,' Markus replied. 'I would prefer bread dumplings, cheese spaetzle, a hearty sausage salad followed by sugared pancakes with raisins.'

'Your Bavarian cuisine also sounds very enticing. What do you think of adding as dessert an additional large piece of cheesecake with cream or Black Forest gateau? At a pinch I would even be content with an entire bar of chocolate.'

'Dude, stop it, Fritz, your imagination is running away with you again. My mouth is watering. And what do we get here apart from hard army bread with weak cold coffee? Only lice, hunger, cold and death.'

Also the topic of girls was by no means forgotten. Uli, Georg, Markus and I often told each other about our longings and desires, since we had never had the opportunity thus far to look for or find our great love, let alone to come closer to a girl physically.

'How would I like to ask the most beautiful girls to dance during events such as the maypole dance, carnival or our parish fair in order to meet someone suitable,' Uli complained bitterly.

'Yet we are sitting here 2,500 kilometres away from home at the arse-end of the world and fear every day for our lives. Just imagine that tomorrow a bullet finds us or a grenade tears us into pieces. That would be it then. Our young lives are wiped out, gone, ex, finis, finito.'

This thought troubled us all and was brought up time and again. To have to die without ever having loved a woman seemed to us the height of cruelty. No, we all wanted to live, return home and not to die. This cast-iron will to survive kept us standing, helped us not to give up, not to resign and, regardless of the horrible present, to look forward with a certain optimism. Our youth helped us to endure the extreme hardships of cold and hunger, the deprivations and the continuous battles. To this was added the bond of a tight-knit comradeship.

Time and again we spoke occasionally about the sense or rather the insanity of this war and questioned most of all our role in this crazy enterprise.

'We find ourselves in a country attacked and largely occupied by us, where none of us ever wanted to go. We bring unspeakable suffering over this people, also the civilian population. Is it not logical and wholly normal that the Russians are fighting us with brute force in order to drive us from their country?' Georg Bauder said to us one evening in the closest circle of comrades. In our tight, bunker-like shelter with sparse candlelight we were luckily among ourselves. Otherwise such utterances could have had fatal consequences.

The Russians showed themselves to be tenacious and relentless adversaries. After the initial successes of the Wehrmacht and the unimaginable losses of the Red Army all the western states would have long since capitulated in order to avoid further bloodshed. Yet capitulation was just as inconceivable for Stalin's reign of terror as a few years later for Hitler's gang of criminals. In order to save their own miserable skin the dictators sacrificed their own peoples without a second thought. In order to defeat them, their states had to be driven to total collapse, as happened with Germany in 1945. Stalin's Russia, however, did not collapse despite the many defeats.

Regardless of the cruel events and the horrible images constantly before our eyes, we felt no hatred for the enemy. On the contrary, the Russian civilian population had always behaved in a friendly manner towards us. Therefore we were by no means willing to lead the war of extermination ordered by the political leadership against the Russian 'sub-humans' or 'Asiatic hordes'. Furthermore, the political propaganda mostly reached us front soldiers only in a weakened form anyway.

One afternoon Lieutenant Engelmann read the following order from division command to the assembled troops:

> During the next interception of an enemy feigned attack in front of our defensive section a counter-attack has to follow immediately beyond the enemy's own positions for the purpose of combatting the enemy. Our objective is the destruction of the enemy units in front of us. The assault will take place en bloc from the entire Regiment 437 upon the appropriate order.

The morning after next we were confronted with this situation. It started with the usual artillery preparation by the Russian 7.6cm division cannons SiS 3, which were called in squaddie slang 'kaboom', because firing and impact could hardly be distinguished acoustically. Once again numerous soldiers, although not in the same masses as in the previous days and weeks, were driven unarmed to their deaths by their commissars – in our eyes unimaginable.

I noticed more and more that the fallen unarmed soldiers showed Asian facial features. At that time I did not know that these were Uzbeks, Tajiks, Azerbaijanis, Kyrgyzs and members of other Turk peoples from the deep south of the Soviet Union. In this manner Stalin decimated by simple means the people of these constituent republics with predominantly Muslim faith, which did not always conform to Moscow. Thus we were basically turned into Stalin's henchmen in his cleansing. In contrast, the soldiers of the Russian provinces were favoured.

When the Russian attack had come to a halt and the enemy started to retreat, the order for the across-the-board attack was given. Officers and corporals shouted almost simultaneously 'Take the high ground', and with at least 200 men we jumped out from our cover and ran towards the enemy, an enemy that was already retreating. All my comrades were there. Across fallen and wounded Red Army soldiers, shell craters, trenches, barbed wire tangles and trees shot to pieces, we hastened forward bent low from cover to cover. The battle noise was deafening, since our forceful carbines 98k made a hell of a noise when fired, likewise the MG 42, not to mention the dull bangs of the hand grenades and mortar shells. Faster and faster we pursued the fleeing Russians, who doggedly defended themselves while retreating.

Again and again we took cover, pressing our faces and bodies into the sheltering soil, then jumped up again on the next command and ran as fast as possible towards the next cover. I was halfway to a depression in the ground, into which I intended to throw myself, and was running as fast as it was possible under the weight of my kit, when I suddenly felt a solid blow on my left thigh. It felt as if somebody had struck a hammer with full force against the inside of my leg. At full speed I fell to the ground, somersaulted and tumbled in several revolutions into a shell crater over which I just had wanted to jump.

After a short while searing pain started up in my left thigh, and both sides of my shot-through uniform trousers were soaked with blood. I screamed for our paramedics. All my comrades were in the process of storming forward or were looking for cover under enemy fire. As many in the regiment knew me, I heard several comrades shouting: 'Fritzje has been hit, Fritzje is wounded.' Some threw me their bandage kits and dived farther forward towards the closest cover. None of my friends and close comrades were near to me.

Upon my shouts for help, my wailing and screaming, somebody whom I only knew fleetingly by sight jumped into the shell crater with me. He talked soothingly to me, took his bayonet from its sheath and with it cut open my uniform trousers and long johns in the region of my twitching and trembling thigh. I saw immediately that a projectile had torn up my left thigh muscle. This time I did not tremble with cold, but with pure terror in every limb.

If the frontal hole was roughly as big as one then Reichsmark, the exit wound was three times as big and bled heavily. Muscle fibre hung in shreds from the gaping wound. Given the searing pain, I was immediately overcome by a terrible fear of losing my leg. The size of the wound meant that it could not have been a normal rifle bullet. We knew that despite the prohibition by the laws of war the enemy occasionally filed off the tips of the projectiles in order to cause serious injuries with these dumdum bullets. The Soviets often also used explosive projectiles. With regards to my wound, it could not have been the latter, though.

My helper had wrapped my open wound with all available bandages in a makeshift fashion. In addition he pulled out his belt and with it put such a strong tourniquet around my leg in my groin area that I screamed in pain. With the words 'we will get you later', he jumped from the crater and vanished in the blink of an eye.

Peering out from the hole, I still saw some comrades running hither and thither in all directions. The battle noise abated and moved away. Yet now I perceived the relative silence as frightening. Suddenly I was lying all alone in this shell crater and held my leg with both hands half sitting, half lying.

Not too far away I heard at least two or three wounded or dying moaning and wheezing, but these horrible sounds finally fell silent, too. I could not discern whether these were Russian soldiers or my own comrades.

What will happen? How will it go on? Who will come and get me? Thousands of thoughts shot through my mind. Could I still crawl and if so into which direction? Here I was lying in no-man's-land somewhere between the front lines. During battle time, space, direction and orientation became blurred. I tried to straighten myself in order to look over the slightly raised rim of the crater. Under this hellish pain it was impossible. Every movement of the leg, however slight, was terribly painful. Immediately I thought of the recently fallen Herbert and longed for my comrades, for Markus, Toni, Walter, Georg and Uli. Where were they at that moment? How had they fared? Were all of them still alive? When would help come? How long would I be able to hang on without medical attention? It was noon, and night fell quickly at this time of the year. Yet in this precarious situation I could only sit and wait.

The dressing had, in the meantime, soaked through. I did not feel any hunger, but aside from the pain was all the more tortured by thirst. The hours passed and they seemed to me like days. It was already getting dark, and my wristwatch showed 5pm. The waiting went on and the pain sapped my fortunately still good physical condition.

When complete darkness had fallen and the temperature had dropped below zero, my hope of rescue by my comrades vanished. Shivering with cold, pain, thirst and fear, I crouched on the ground hunched over and stared into the night. Meanwhile, I told myself quietly again and again: 'Do not close your eyes and fall asleep, you must stay awake. Do not fall asleep, do not give up!'

Around midnight I heard the voices of patrols and reconnaissance parties from different directions, who were probably looking for wounded or dead soldiers in order to recover them. While Russian sounds were constantly heard in my immediate vicinity, for a short while I believed I heard German voices farther away. Yet because of the Russians close by I did not dare call for help.

The squaddie who had treated me had promised to instigate my recovery and rescue and to bring me back from this hole. Yet perhaps he himself had fallen in the battle, and nobody knew of my injury. Did anyone even suspect me to be still alive, or had they given up on me? During the night I heard battle noise everywhere, and I saw tracer bullets whizzing overhead. This night was full of activities, and numerous flares lightened the night sky. From various directions salvoes clattered from machine pistols and machine guns.

This night became the longest and worst of my life. Countless times I prayed the Lord's Prayer and asked God for help. My entire life in all its facets passed through my thoughts. My late father, my mother, my brothers Hans, Peter and Karl suddenly felt so close to me. During this night my great dream of taking part in the Olympic Games had been shattered forever. I sensed the injury, the blood loss, the cold and the thirst eat away my strength. A creeping, slowly approaching weakness overcame me. At dawn I believed I was no longer myself, but the horrific night was finally over. I was already too weak for crawling. It was now just waiting for my comrades or for certain death.

As of now my thoughts were still clear and not confused. With all my might I wanted to live and tried to stay awake. Yet how long could I hang on before my senses deteriorated? I dug up my emergency ration, which every squaddie carried around in his uniform pocket for months, if not years. It was a punishable offence to eat this without compelling reasons, but I decided that this emergency had occurred, and I greedily ate the 'Scho-ka-kola' containing caffeine. When the darkness finally receded, new hope arose in me. Despite the immense pain and the hellish thirst, I was determined to win the battle against weakness and fatigue. You must not fall asleep! This I told myself over and over. Do not fall asleep now and freeze to death!

When my gaze fell onto my wristwatch for the last time, it was already 9am. My strength was spent, and I noticed the desire for eternal sleep rising inside me. Only subconsciously at first, I heard quiet voices, then commands and immediately after quick steps. What I was seeing now, brought tears to my eyes despite my lack of strength. I saw how Lieutenant Engelmann and Corporal Kleinschmidt secured the area with machine pistols at the ready, while Markus, Toni, Georg and Uli jumped into the crater with me. I saw a paramedic with a Red Cross armlet and in his wake four Russian volunteers with a stretcher.

'My God, Fritz, finally we have found you!' my comrades called to me deeply worried, when they saw me lying in my miserable state. 'We were looking for you yesterday evening at nightfall, but were harassed and shot at by Russian reconnaissance parties. We did not manage to get through to you. We will bring you back. You can do this, hang on!'

I sensed the stretcher being lifted up. The first hundred metres were negotiated at a jog in spite of the difficult terrain. I could not recall the remainder of the rescue mission.

8

On the Ambulance Train back to the Reich

Roughly two hours later I was woken up shortly before arriving at the large main dressing station of the 132nd Infantry Division by ungentle rocking atop a transport for the wounded. I saw that I was lying next to three other grievously injured soldiers who were moaning loudly. The accompanying medical orderly looked at me and said in surprise:

> Don't say that you did not notice the shootout! Although we are marked with the Red Cross, the Ivans have pelted us with artillery. One of our four trucks received a direct hit. Driver, accompanying personnel and wounded – all dead! We almost croaked it shortly before our destination, too. We were extremely damned lucky!

Immediately after our arrival at the main dressing station we were carefully unloaded from the truck. Covered with a woollen blanket against the cold, we were put down in a row beside a tent with a Red Cross flag at its peak. It was a relatively large surgery tent, which was very busy. Patiently we were lying on our stretchers and waited for our treatment. I was in third place and from my spot could look behind the tent. There, between two trees at a distance of less than 15 metres, twenty dead soldiers were lying. They had been piled up like logs and were at that moment carried away one by one by a rescue team.

When I was finally carried into the surgery tent, two paramedics placed me gently on one of the two operating tables, still partly smeared with blood. Immediately an older, but agile senior field doctor with the rank of a lieutenant colonel approached me. Instantly he had a calming effect on me. Carefully he removed my blood-soaked dressing, and horrified I stared at my shredded thigh. I looked at blood-smeared surgical instruments, various hand saws for amputations and containers on the ground containing cut off hands, feet, arms and legs.

A terrible fear rose inside me, and I implored the doctor: 'Please, please save my leg!'

He asked me in a calm voice: 'What is your name, where do you come from and what is your profession?'

'My name is Fritz Sauer, come from the Coblenz area in the Rhineland and I am a hairdresser. I have to stand the whole day and urgently need my two legs for this. In addition I am a competitive sportsman. May I keep my leg? Please, please, do not amputate it!' I replied.

The friendly doctor nodded and said: 'We do not amputate that quickly. We will try everything to save your leg.'

Out of relief I broke into tears. With my eighteen years I was lying mewling and helpless on the operating table of a field hospital. Without any facial hair yet apart from a slight blond fuzz, I must have seemed half a child to him. And while I continued to look around anxiously and tensely, I observed something that has remained stuck in my memory until today: shortly before the anaesthesia took hold, I just glimpsed how tears were running down the face of the old senior field doctor. Certainly he had experienced thousands of worse injuries before my surgery, young soldiers whose lives he could not save any more. This doctor cried for me though, for whatever reason. Perhaps he was crying for a young generation whom he saw bleeding out in a criminal war.

I woke up on a rolling railway wagon, to be precise on a Russian goods wagon, lying on straw next to many other wounded, some of whom were moaning loudly. The train brought us quickly out from the front area. My first glance went immediately down to my legs, and I saw both my feet. Thank God, my leg had been saved and was held in a kind of traction bandage. We were lying on a train towards the Lithuanian–German border accompanied by some paramedics, but without further medical treatment. There was a pungent smell of blood-soaked dressings, urine and faeces, but the food was adequate throughout the journey.

At the Lithuanian–German border our final stop for now was the German small town of Wirballen (modern Virbalis in Lithuania). The train was unloaded, and the wounded brought into the station building. In a large room we had to undress ourselves, for the largest part with the aid of the nursing staff, and everybody was washed and deloused as far as his injuries permitted. To this procedure also belonged the disinfection of all items of clothing, as well as the genitals.

Nobody who has not experienced this can imagine the sight of this huge room! Everything was covered in blood and excrement. It smelled horrible – a stench of human misery and death. Moaning and screams of pain echoed through the room. Many brave comrades endured their suffering without complaint. I saw amputees missing arms, feet and legs, lung shots, stomach shots, head shots, neck shots, severe eye injuries and men whose faces had been disfigured beyond recognition by shrapnel or burns. A grotesque, indescribable sight presented itself to our eyes, and dramatic scenes were played out. It looked like a giant abattoir for humans. Was this hell's precipice or the place that led out of hell?

After this undeniably necessary procedure we were brought gently but quickly to the opposite exit of the station, where a train was waiting ready to depart – a wonderful sight full of hope. Before us stood an endlessly long ambulance train equipped with the most modern couchette coaches of the Reichsbahn. Embarkation followed without noteworthy delays. The serious and most serious casualties received a freshly made bed on the couchette coaches. Throughout the entire train well-trained paramedics and Red Cross nurses were stationed. Even a young nun and a priest were present. In addition, a senior field doctor took care of the patients. After a short time we travelled towards Königsberg, now on the European normal track rail network. There the first most serious casualties were unloaded for further treatment. The rapid journey continued through the now deeply snowed in East Prussia, then West Prussia and further deep into Reich territory.

Most of the wounded received new dressings during the journey and adequate nourishment. Every patient was wearing a marching slip around his neck on which personal information as well as the manner and severity of the injury were noted. In addition, the patient's destination was given. On the train selections were made in a rapid and uncomplicated manner so that the soldiers could be transferred to those field hospitals and regular hospitals that offered the best treatment for their injuries. There were even special clinics for facial surgery for those mutilated in part beyond recognition. My destination was listed as a field hospital in Lippstadt in Westphalia.

The train drove full steam ahead towards the west and only stopped in big cities to bunker water and coal for the locomotive. In order not to lose time, twice express locomotives under steam were hitched up. For many of the most severe casualties time was pressing, as there was only limited availability of the intensive treatment required for them on board. At almost every stop some comrades who had succumbed to their injuries during travel were lifted from the wagons. Presumably the poor lads were buried in close-by military cemeteries.

At every stop Red Cross nurses were waiting on the platforms to pass us warm soup, chocolate, cigarettes and further provisions through the open carriage windows. We wounded experienced an incredible solidarity, also on the part of the civilian population. Time and again people on platforms waved or slipped us little gifts through the open windows. It was truly astonishing how smoothly the war machine and the care for the wounded were still functioning in November 1942. During the war years, 500 ambulance trains were running continuously, bringing wounded of all fronts home. To these were added patients who were flown out in Ju 52 transport planes.

At the end of 1942 wounded German soldiers on average received their final treatment after eighteen hours. In light of these large distances from the front and the inexhaustible masses of thousands upon thousands of casualties this was a top-class logistical performance.

During those November days of 1942 Hitler had reached the summit of his power after more than three years of war. From the Atlantic Ocean to Mount Elbrus in the Caucasus, from Norway across the Balkans to Greece and Crete, his sphere of influence ranged, and soldiers of the Wehrmacht were even present in North Africa. To these were added the ships of the navy and hundreds of submarines, which made life difficult for the maritime transports of the Allies.

Yet exactly at that time when I was on my train journey from hell towards Lippstadt, the tides of the course of the Second World War were turning. A terrible tribute was paid at all fronts to this megalomania. Hitler had over-reached himself. Germany and its armed forces could no longer cope with the pressure they themselves had created.

On 19 November 1942 near Kalach the Red Army closed the cauldron around the 6th Army under Colonel General Friedrich Paulus – which with twenty-two divisions and 250,000 men was the strongest German army at the Eastern Front. The Afrika Korps under Field Marshal Erwin Rommel could no longer withstand the superior forces of the Allies, who consisted of British, New Zealanders, Australians, South Africans and Americans, and was equally lost. Almost the entire Korps ended up as prisoners of war and was interned in Camp Shelby in the Mississippi swamps or in Canada.

The navy had to report great losses, too, especially of submarines, after the British had succeeded in breaking the German encryption codes, and the Luftwaffe lost far more than half of its transport planes during the African operation and the supply of the Stalingrad pocket. It could offer less and less opposition against the increasingly stronger British and American bomber fleets, and even above Germany air superiority was lost. The losses among the civilian population grew dramatically, and damage to industrial complexes impeded the production of armaments.

Of all these events we simple soldiers did not know any details, and what we learned came from unfounded rumours. Yet we had learned to read between the lines of newspapers and letters, and from the totality of the news, complemented by casualty reports and rumours, arose pieces of the puzzle that we combined to form a more or less accurate picture of the true war situation.

The prognosis of my amiable regiment commander during our journey to the Crimea that only a miracle would be able to save Germany from inevitable defeat was confirmed to me after my own experiences at the front. Miracles only happen rarely!

Having arrived at Lippstadt with some other soldiers, I was carried from the train, which was now only transporting a few casualties, and immediately continued towards its final destination, Essen. In military ambulances we were taken immediately to the local hospital, which had been operating as a reserve field hospital since 15 February 1940 and was subordinated to the military sanitary centre at Münster. In this hospital, 120 beds were provided for serious casualties.

In the field hospital we were treated promptly and professionally. The further examinations and treatment by the doctors and care attendants was impeccable. Finally, I was accommodated in a four-bed room.

The first nights I slept like in paradise in the clean white hospital bed in spite of the pain in the wound. The feeling of having escaped the Eastern Front with its thousands of fatal dangers, its suffering and its hardships was overwhelming and cannot be described in words. Yet we were all traumatised to varying degrees by the events and the horrible images that followed us into our dreams. Time and gain the screams of comrades waking from nightmares resounded through the echoing corridors.

It took until shortly before Christmas before I could carefully tread onto the injured left leg for the first time and risk putting some pressure on it. Until then I had been mostly confined to my bed or had tried occasionally to hop on the right leg supported by two crutches.

In the neighbouring room I regularly visited Uwe Andres, with whom I had struck up a friendship. His personal background, his stories and especially his care were interesting. Uwe was a dive bomber pilot and flew a Ju 87. He told me:

> On the return flight from a combat mission with the Army Group Centre we were shot at by a Polikarpov I-16 fighter plane with its on-board weapons. In this process not only was our plane shot out from under our backsides, but my actual backside as well. Severely injured, I was just able to save myself by parachute at the last minute, but my on-board mechanic and combat observer on the back seat received several hits. He was killed immediately and crashed with our burning aircraft.

If you will forgive my vulgarity, Uwe's arse was literally blown off. Fortunately his anus had remained intact, but where the two buttocks had been was now an ugly open wound. I was often present when one of the nurses powdered and dressed his backside. Afterwards Uwe was arranged onto a pumped up truck tyre so that no pressure was exerted onto the remains of his backside. This method, born out of necessity, contributed much to lessening his pain and to further healing.

The food in the field hospital was remarkably good. Finally we could wash ourselves regularly again, too, and had time to ourselves

It was ironic. In spite of our serious injuries we were doing relatively well in the field hospital. We listened daily to the news about Stalingrad on the radio, and as now experienced front soldiers we recognised between the lines the hopelessness of the situation and the looming downfall. How bad will these poor comrades have fared at a time when we were lying in relative peace in a hospital at home! Compared to this human tragedy, whose full extent only became apparent in later years, the almost daily bombing raids, especially on the Ruhr region with its heavy industry, seemed just as bad, but not quite as unbearable.

Shortly before Christmas I received mail from Mother. She intended to visit me here in Lippstadt after Christmas and the bitterly cold winter full of snow.

In the days before Christmas the mood in the hospital turned melancholic. Many patients were discharged, and homesickness plagued those who had to stay. I had to remain in the field hospital, too, since the healing process still took time.

They tried to make the holidays as pleasant as possible for those who had to spend Christmas in the hospital. They did arts and crafts, decorated and baked biscuits and Christmas stollen cake. It seemed as if peace on earth had become a reality, and suddenly there was no longer any smell of ether, chloroform, blood, pus, disinfectants and other horrible things, but of cinnamon, gingerbread, ginger nuts, and almonds – it smelled like Christmas.

On Christmas Eve our hearts became heavy, especially those who had been marked for life – young men of just around twenty years old whose limbs had been amputated.

We spent the afternoon of Christmas Eve together in the great hall. We listened to the musical request concert on the radio with many Christmas songs and the intermittent greetings to soldiers on all fronts.

In the late afternoon we were all seized by sentimentality, and we thought of home. No later than during the song 'Homeland, Your Stars' the first, painstakingly suppressed tears were flowing. The subsequent great Christmas circular programme transmitted throughout the whole of Europe by the Greater German Broadcasting Company was followed by an audience of millions. They continually jumped between the various theatres of war, and participants from the Northern Cape down to Africa, from the Atlantic Ocean to Stalingrad got a chance to speak. It was a propaganda programme staged with huge effort that conjured up with stirring emotions the solidarity of the great German national community even in hard times. This was very cleverly arranged, and at the end when the three verses of the probably most beautiful German Christmas song 'Silent Night' were played, all dams were breaking. Everybody got all dewy eyed and nobody was ashamed of his tears.

At the beginning of February Mother visited me, again accompanied by Aunt Anna. With what exertions did the two older women put up with for this! This was no journey like the year before into the Western Palatinate to Baumholder. No, here deepest winter still held sway, and our country, especially railway lines, train stations and big cities, were subject to constant bombing raids. Their journey led them to Lippstadt with changes in Coblenz, Cologne and Dortmund. It was a happy reunion, although my mother had suffered a panic attack when while changing trains she had suddenly lost sight of her sister in the hustle of the completely overcrowded Dortmund station, as Aunt Anna recounted. The matter luckily ended well, after the two found each other in time to continue the journey and could board the train to Lippstadt.

Naturally I was pleased with the little gifts they had brought me, but much more I was glad about our first reunion after nine months. Mother immediately took a look at my leg, whose healing process was progressing rather slowly. Without crutches walking was still not possible.

She immediately told me about a strange incident that had occurred at the end of last year: 'Just imagine, my boy. In the middle of a cold November night the large wooden cross with Holy Jesus fell from the wall by itself in my bedroom. Frightened and full of panic, I spontaneously spoke aloud: My God, now something has happened to our Fritz. For the rest of the night I no longer found any rest due to my agitation.'

'When exactly did this happen, Mother?' I asked astonished.

We did the maths together and came to the conclusion that it must have been the same night during which I had lain wounded in the shell crater. It might have had significance or been only a coincidence. At that moment, however, my faith in God became even more steadfast, since I now had confirmation that my prayers not had been in vain during the worst situations and somehow had been heard.

We talked for a long time and in detail, for there was much news but only a small part of it was good. The tragedy of Stalingrad with the demise of the 6th Army weighed on many of us, since we almost all had relatives and acquaintances who were enclosed in the pocket. The fate of some of the other men from our village were tied up with it. No sign of life had been received from them any longer, and they were considered missing. Among others, my cousin Heinrich Sauer had been lost there. The uncertainty of his death was depressing for my aunt and uncle and the entire family. Had he starved, frozen to death, been shot or torn apart? Nobody could ever give information about his fate to the mourning parents and relatives.

Mother told me further about the raid by a thousand bombers of the Royal Air Force on Cologne. 'Imagine that, Fritz, after the city had been so heavily bombed, many helpers had been ordered there. Also, many older men from our village were sent there by the local group leader Servatius for clearing work in the city 100 kilometres away. What the returning men then told us was dreadful. The beautiful cathedral city was an unimaginable wasteland in the historic part,' she continued. 'The corpses of the civilian population were lying piled metres high on the pavements for days, until they could be carted away and in part be buried in mass graves.'

I immediately had to think of Jakob Schmitz, who had returned after his lung wound to his home city that had already been destroyed. How would he have fared? Where would he have gone?

Then Mother gave an account on a bombing raid on Coblenz and the matter of my brother Hans' draft. Although the latter had been put down as deferred from military service due to our farm and the front deployment of two brothers – Peter and I – he was drafted instead of the baker Karl Riegel. The matter was quickly recounted. Actually, Riegel was supposed to be drafted according to the enlisting order but he donated a cow to the NSDAP local group leader Servatius. The latter accepted the gift gladly, but still had to deliver the number of recruits demanded by the Wehrmacht. And so he sent our Hans, who did not stoop to an attempt at bribery. So simple was the matter at that time.

Karl continued to maintain the farm and worked the fields, now only with the Polish prisoner of war after the French guy had fled during one night and had probably found his way back to France on foot.

In autumn during the potato harvest another alarming incident took place and this time it concerned Karl. He spent days harvesting potatoes with the Polish labourer. There were no machines, and thus all the potatoes had to be dug up by hand, filled into the 50kg sacks and loaded onto the cart. Tired from the heavy labour, Karl and his Polish companion had fallen asleep after lunch under a tree in the neighbouring cherry orchard. Suddenly local group leader Servatius appeared holding a riding crop and roared something about 'subverters of the war effort and layabouts'. Finally he said to Karl: 'I will get rid of you as well!'

With these words he vanished as quickly as he had come.

Whether it was this scene or an incident that had happened in the course of the deportation of the local Jews – my mother did not know what had antagonised the local group leader so much against our family.

'It happened on that day when the two Jewish families in Bassenheim were picked up and transported to the train station for deportation to Coblenz,' my mother told me, visibly moved.

She realised that they were just about to load the Heimann family from Mayener Straße and the Simon family living in Charlottenstraße onto an open truck. Among those to be deported were also the three boys of the latter family, Manfred, Siegfried and Norbert. Siegfried had been my classmate and Norbert went to school with Karl. How often these Jewish children had been at our home in the past and had played with us! Karl, who had no bicycle of his own, was allowed to ride around on Siegfried's red or Norbert's blue bike as he pleased. Mother was very worried about the fate of the Jewish neighbour families. Full of pity, she spontaneously made several sandwiches as food for the journey and sent seventeen-year-old Karl to Charlottenstraße with them. When the boy wanted to hand the sandwiches to the family on the truck, Servatius, who was monitoring the operation, approached and kicked all the sandwiches out of Karl's hands so that they fell into the dirt of the unpaved road.

Deeply disappointed and depressed, Karl trotted back home and described this incident to Mother. This was a disgraceful and inhumane crime unfolding of whose full extent we were not aware yet at that time though. Officially it was said that the Jews were taken to special labour camps. Nobody suspected then that the deportation was the beginning of the cruel journey towards the Holocaust – the darkest chapter in German history and perhaps of human history. Nothing was ever heard of either family again.

Finally, Mother told me in tears that my good childhood friend, Edgar Weiber, had fallen two weeks ago.

This news saddened me no end and moved me deeply. 'My God, Mother, the bad news has no end any more. What would I have liked to tell Edgar! I will miss him very much.'

The two women were allowed to have dinner with me and beyond that to spend the night in the hospital. The next morning they left early to travel back to Bassenheim on the overcrowded Reichsbahn trains.

After my leg had healed so far that I could walk again, albeit still limping noticeably, I was discharged at the beginning of May for two weeks' leave at home. I carried my marching orders in my luggage for a convalescent company in Saarburg near Lorraine.

I enjoyed the journey on the overcrowded trains. It was an indescribably lofty feeling not to travel to any front, but to my beloved home which I had not seen since a year.

When the train pulled up in the heavily damaged main station of Cologne, I saw for the first time the full extent of the deep scars on the city. The historic town now consisted almost only of ruins and debris. In the middle of it stood the Gothic cathedral of Cologne, coal black and damaged by bombs, fire and soot, but still steadfast. It seemed like a relic from another, better time, a symbol of hope that gave support and strength to the people in order to continue living.

Only the onward journey through the romantic Rhine valley in full bloom, past Bonn, Bad Godesberg, Remagen, Sinzig, Bad Bresig and Andernach to Coblenz pushed the horrific images of the once so magnificent cathedral city of Cologne from my mind, and I took pleasure in the familiar sight of home.

9

Convalescent Battalion, Saarburg, Lorraine

What I found upon arrival home was not very encouraging. Mother seemed depressed and worried. The house and farm did not give a good impression and were in a worse condition than the year before. At least the fields had been tilled to some extent, for whenever Hans or Peter were on home leave, they helped out at home and on the farm. Also the siblings of my parents, especially Mother's brother Gottfried, helped as much as it was possible for them.

Only my brother Karl was not present. When I asked Mother after his whereabouts, she told me glumly and in agitation what had happened during the most recent weeks: Karl had received his draft notice in which it was written that he had to proceed immediately to Munich for the formation of the newly established 12th SS Tank Division 'Hitler Youth'. Uncle Gottfried had travelled with him to the responsible Military District Command in Wiesbaden immediately after the arrival of the draft notice. Their attempt to request Karl's deployment elsewhere failed. The reasoning that Karl had not volunteered, that he was the last son on the farm, that he worked with his single mother, that three brothers were already soldiers and that this was certainly a mistake produced little effect. They had come down like a ton of bricks on him there after he had been shown a written recommendation for this deployment, signed by Servatius. A few days later Karl had packed his things into an old cardboard box, and following the draft notice, had travelled to Munich to his unit. Since then she had not received any news from him.

The next days I tried, as far as my weakened leg permitted, to help out on the farm together with our Polish labourer. Twice a week I had to report for after treatment to our head doctor Dr Sauvigny at our hospital. I recovered quite well during those two weeks and could get some of the pending tasks done.

Shortly before the end of this leave I travelled into Coblenz by train in order to get some necessary equipment there. At the same time I had some photos taken of me in uniform at the photo studio Stiebel. During my walk through town I had a miraculous encounter. Suddenly, in the middle of Löhrstraße, my comrade Josef Reif from Dieblich was standing before me. It was incredible! We had heard nothing of each other since I had been wounded and my transport back to Germany. He had come a few days before from the front at the Volkhov River and was now likewise on leave. What a reunion! We embraced each other cordially and told each other about our experiences. My closest comrades were fortunately all still alive, however nothing had been heard of Georg Bauder from Mannheim since he had disappeared on a reconnaissance patrol mission. The entire party of four men was missing.

When the first early cherries were ripening in the Rhine Valley, my wonderful time on leave drew to a close. Josef returned to the front and the 132nd Infantry Division in Russia and I travelled, as stated in my marching orders, to the aforementioned convalescent battalion in Saarburg (French Sarreguemines in Lorraine, not to be confused with the town Saarburg near Trier and Konz).

I was accommodated there in a barrack with slightly and moderately injured soldiers, and here we effectively experienced our physical training anew and our reintegration into the Wehrmacht. My injury was classified as moderate with impaired mobility.

Almost every front division had such convalescent battalions at that time in which the convalescent soldiers were made fit for the next front deployment. After a pretty much complete recovery of their operational readiness, these soldiers were restored to the original units as reserves – as far as the latter still existed.

The daily routine ran a similar course to the one in the previous year at the Gneisenau barracks in Coblenz, except that all the participants in this bunch including the numerous instructors were already marked by war, sometimes more, sometimes less.

I wore the black Badge of the Wounded with some pride on my uniform jacket, but there were several squaddies among us who had already received the silver or even the golden Badge of the Wounded, signifying that they had been wounded on several occasions. This was no longer the young, healthy and dynamic gang as it was the year before prior to our first deployment.

Many of our comrades were half cripples, although the very severely wounded were no longer drafted to the reserves. Nevertheless, training and duty followed the usual strict military procedures. The more critical the situations became at the far-stretched fronts and through the continuous heavy bombing raids on the cities, the rougher and harsher the tone became in the barracks.

In the middle of 1943 a great tank battle occurred in the central section of the Eastern Front. The military situation during this summer presented the following picture: The turn of the year and spring 1943 were marked by the serious defeat at Stalingrad, as already mentioned, and the subsequent victory of German SS units in Kharkov. Nevertheless, the Wehrmacht found itself on the defensive. Its almost 160 divisions, which were however very weakened in parts, were confronted along the 2,500 kilometres of front by almost 400 major units of the Red Army. A loss of initiative was threatening and thus the danger of entering into a battle of attrition with the more numerous and materially superior Red Army, which had already lost around 11 million men in the previous years of war but nonetheless became continually stronger.

After its initial setbacks the Soviet Union had mobilised all its forces in the preceding two years of war. The entire country was working for the front under the dictatorial leadership of the Communist Party. Almost Russia's entire industry had been adjusted to the wartime economy. The armament factories, successfully evacuated to the hinterland during the first months of the war, produced an ever increasing number of tanks, aircraft and ordnance. To these were added the aforementioned significant deliveries of weapons and equipment by the United States and Britain under the Lend-Lease Agreement. In addition, millions of potential recruits of draft age were available in spite of the enormous losses. It was only a matter of time before the more abundant resources in comparison to Germany and most of all the continually intensifying armament industry would tip the balance in favour of the Soviet Union.

With the increasing material strength the abilities of the Soviet armed forces on the battlefield had improved, too, especially the ability for strategic operations. Powerful tank and aerial armies were created that successfully met with the still well-equipped and experienced Wehrmacht. The quality of the leading personnel had improved. The bloody pre-war purges within the officer corps of the Red Army were partly responsible for the devastating defeats at the beginning of the war, but they had cleared the path for a younger generation. Especially in the higher leadership levels, officers were now called into action who on average were almost twenty years younger than their German opponents. They had learned their craft by doing, modelled on the successful operations of the Wehrmacht. Now they relied increasingly on active, dynamic warfare and the thorough deception of the adversary. Furthermore, the practice of uncoordinated frontal assaults that had been common in many places during 1941/42 and had led to enormous losses for the Red Army was finally given up.

The German High Command failed to a large extent to recognise this dramatic development, most of all Hitler who saw himself confirmed in his assessment of our own possibilities due to the preceding success of the SS divisions during the reconquest of Kharkov and who still underestimated the opponent. Although some voices pleaded for a cautious attitude and the preparation of a counter-offensive against a large-scale attack by the Red Army to be expected sooner or later, in the end the advocates of a German summer offensive of their own prevailed. In particular Hitler, who urgently needed a decisive victory in view of the political and military developments, supported an aggressive approach. So he stated several times that he had no time to wait for Stalin in the light of the unfolding development in other theatres of war.

An obvious goal for a limited German summer offensive was the 'Kursk Bulge'. This was the already mentioned front protrusion of the Red Army that had arisen from the battles at the beginning of 1943 and which reached deep into the German lines.

The aim of the operation hence consisted in binding the strong Soviet offensive forces present in the wider area of Kursk through a rapid pincer movement and if possible encircling them. Subsequently the Soviet forces were to be worn down in an encirclement battle. With this the Soviet Union would have been robbed of the forces required for a large-scale offensive. After that the German High Command wanted to regain the initiative at the Eastern Front if possible.

Therefore the operation was an offensive, but served the defence and was supposed to hinder the advance of the Soviet Union. Such great losses were to be inflicted upon the Red Army that at least for the following months no large-scale attacks on the German front could be expected. The German

High Command further hoped to free up at least ten armoured units with the intended shortening of the front. These troops were to be deployed to other theatres of war, especially against the threatening Allied invasion of Italy and Western Europe. With this a real strategic reserve was supposed to be created for the first time. The aim of the Wehrmacht command was now to offer such successful resistance against the Allies that they would be ready for a peace agreement that would leave at least part of the previously conquered territories with Germany.

The operation plan was based on an idea of the commander of Army Group South, General Field Marshal Erich von Manstein, which he had developed after the successful reconquest of Kharkov. The plan received the cover name Operation Citadel and was laid down in the orders of the Army High Command no. 5 dated 13 March 1943 and no. 6 dated 15 April 1943.

The Kursk Bulge at the front line had an approximate side length of 200 kilometres and a depth of up to 150 kilometres. The plan intended to mount the offensive from both sides at the foot of the bulge and to cut off all Soviet troops gathered in the frontal protrusion from their main front. The operative goal was the city of Kursk, where the two spearheads were supposed to meet up on the fifth or sixth day of the offensive. After the breakthrough had ensued, during the second phase the encircled Soviet troops and their reserves – in total eight to ten armies – were to be destroyed.

The plan was conventional, aimed at bringing about a classical cauldron battle and hence corresponded to the known previous approach famed under the synonym Blitzkrieg [lightning war]. Therefore one could hardly count on an element of surprise. The success was supposed to be forced through mainly with the aid of the concentrated deployment of armoured troops and new weapons systems in both main thrusts.

For the operation, in the north with Army Group Centre under General Field Marshal Günther von Kluge, the 9th Army (General Walter Model) with twenty-two divisions including eight tank and mechanised infantry divisions was made available. The Army Group South under von Manstein concentrated the 5th Tank Army and an army detachment ('Kempf') with nineteen divisions in total, among them nine tank and mechanised infantry divisions, in the southern section. To the 4th Tank Army under Hermann Hoth also belonged the 2nd SS Tank Corps under Senior Group Leader Paul Hausser with the three mechanised infantry divisions 'Leibstandarte Adolf Hitler', 'The Reich' and 'Death Head'. The aerial fleets Four and Six, likewise made available and which were supposed to cooperate closely with the ground forces, were reinforced by aerial forces from other sections of the front. In total 2,000 aircraft, among them improved models of the Heinkel He 111 (bomber), Focke-Wulf Fw 190 (fighter/fighter-bomber) and Henschel Hs 129 (ground attack) were to support the assault by the ground forces.

In spite of these enormous concentrations of troops, the plan suffered from a decisive flaw that had already led to the failure of the large-scale offensives of 1942 in the Caucasus and at Stalingrad: the necessary forces and means for its successful implementation were simply lacking. In particular there was a lack of troops that were to be brought up as reinforcements to cover the flanks of the spearheads. It was therefore impossible to schedule the defensive battle at the flanks of the attacking forces, which was supposed to follow the advance according to the plan. Thus the latter troops had to face up to this task themselves instead of concentrating all forces on the advance. The decisive forces were thus involved in skirmishes of attrition and lost their strike capability, which in the end led to the failure of the operation.

Some of those responsible at the High Command and at the front were aware of the discrepancy between plan and reality. Some were convinced that the window of opportunity for the success of the operation – already postponed several times – had already closed as the adversary had gained in strength and was waiting for the attack in well-established and deeply staggered defensive systems. However, they could not assert themselves against the advocates and especially Hitler as Supreme Commander of the Wehrmacht. Hitler saw the armoured arm as the decisive factor on the battlefield. He therefore expected that success would come about in any case with the massive deployment of the new tank models.

After the fall of Tunisia to the Allied troops and the resulting total loss of the Afrika Korps – a military disaster numerically comparable in its extent to Stalingrad, although under less atrocious circumstances – Hitler postponed the beginning of Citadel on 13 May to the end of June in view of the now real threat to German-occupied Greece or even to Italy by an Allied landing operation on Sicily. Hitler first wanted to be certain that Fascist Italy would continue the war after the loss of its North African colonies and while being faced with a tangible threat, before he approved a massive deployment of troops at the Eastern Front.

The development in North Africa was not the only factor though: most critical were the massive logistical difficulties in the area of Army Group

Centre, which were caused by extensive partisan activities in the Orel region, as well as further demands for reinforcements. The commander of the 9th Army and commander of the northern attack wing, Walter Model, stood out in this latter respect. Although Model had time and again argued in favour of Citadel in front of Hitler, this behaviour was posthumously often interpreted as a sign of his hidden opposition to the plan.

The partisan units operating in the dense forests east of the Desna River and in the rear of the 9th Army and 2nd Tank Army were led centrally by the Soviet High Command and massively supported by air with weapons, equipment and personnel. They included, according to current estimates, more than 100,000 men that spring. Their attacks and acts of sabotage had taken on such a scale that the railway capacities, already inadequate in any case, were even further restricted. Therein was a real risk for the implementation of Citadel, for which not only the connecting roads on the North–South axis were expanded, but also the network of bridges in order to transport the new heavy Ferdinand anti-tank vehicles to the front. The Wehrmacht began large-scale operations against the partisans in May and these lasted several weeks. Several front units intended for Citadel – among them an especially effective unit, the 4th Tank Division – were involved.

On 10 July 1943 the Allied landing on Sicily took place, for which reason the offensive of the southern group of the German Wehrmacht at the Eastern Front and hence Operation Citadel had to be terminated at Hitler's behest once and for all in view of the operational situation. The core units of the assault troops were transferred to other theatres of war, among others to the Soviet offensive in the Orel region, which began on 12 July. There Soviet attack forces in coordinated collaboration with large partisan units, which had prepared for months for this day, breached the weak German lines of the 2nd Tank Army and achieved a breakthrough of around 20 kilometres in depth.

The danger arose of a breakthrough towards Orel and of an encirclement of the advanced 9th Army. Therefore the only possibility remaining to the German attack forces was to cease the already mired attack towards Kursk without delay and to swing towards the north with the reserve divisions. The aim of Citadel to encircle and destroy a large part of the Soviet forces con-centrated in the Kursk Bulge had thus become unachievable. Nevertheless, fierce battles ensued on this section of the front.

In spite of the stable situation in the area of Army Group South, its spearheads were withdrawn on 18 July to their initial positions without enemy pressure. The core units were detailed somewhere else. The division 'Greater Germany' was deployed to the Orel region for the support of the 2nd Tank Army, and the 2nd SS Tank Corps was to be transferred to Italy in order to be deployed against the Allied invasion in southern Italy. The escalating events at the Eastern Front allowed only for the transfer of the division 'Leibstandarte'. The troops remaining in Army Group South at this section of the front had to confront the Russian offensive Rumyantsev, which began on 5 August.

For the Soviet side, however, the battle near Kursk had in no way ended. They saw their own attacks brought forth as a reaction to Citadel only as the prelude for their sweeping offensive efforts in summer 1943. From 3 August onwards the reconquest of the region around Kharkov began. By the end of September the Red Army had crossed the Dnieper and repulsed the Army Group South far back.

The losses in men and material through the continuous, attritional military operations into which the German Reich had manoeuvred itself could no longer be compensated in the long run. Everything steered towards great disaster and defeat, although propaganda began to spread rallying calls like a mantra and to invoke the final victory.

Far away from the front we heard here in sleepy Saarburg rather little of all the dramatic events and the escalating developments. Apart from a few incidents and despite our handicaps the usual barrack duty was at any rate a thousand times more bearable than deployment at the front.

One of these negative incidents was an argument with Senior Lieutenant Großmann. The latter was perhaps not actually a fanatical firebrand, but in spite of his disability after an amputation of his forearm he was an especially ambitious instructor. When he chased us over the obstacle course in the grounds and I faltered at climbing over the two-metre high boarded wall due to my infirm leg, I received a loud and coarse admonition. However, my once so strong left take-off leg did not work as it had used to, and a quick run-up was only possible to a very limited and restricted extent.

Yet due to my front experience and my callousness gained in the meantime he did not achieve the desired intimidation with me. Athletically I would have easily put him in the shade, and so I replied coldly: 'That your arm was amputated, Senior Lieutenant Sir, is immediately noticeable, my thigh injury in contrast is not.'

I limped leisurely around the obstacle and simply left the officer standing there. Sometime later he apologised to me in a private conversation, and with this the incident was forgotten.

At the end of the second week I experienced an incredible event: during morning muster we were informed that all newcomers of the last fortnight had to report at 1pm after lunch in front of the staff building. Right on the time ordered about fifty to sixty soldiers were standing there when our sergeant major introduced an older lieutenant colonel of the reserve from the military district command Saarbrücken. This good-natured and rather fatherly man, in my estimation almost 60 years old, greeted us with calm and cordial words. He only had one question for us, he explained, and he apologised that we had been told to report especially because of him. However, he said that because of a specific matter he had been visiting the battalion regularly. Then he asked:

> Can one of you provide me with information about the fate of my son who served in the 437th Regiment of the 132nd Infantry Division and perhaps was at the front together with you? I would like to learn more about the circumstances of his injury and death. My fallen son's name is Herbert Niederländer. Whoever has any information regarding this, please step up.

I received a stab through the heart. I became weak-kneed, and this tragedy, now already months in the past, ran like a bad film before my eyes again, I stepped forward to this visibly moved man, who was Herbert's father.

'Private Fritz Sauer, Lieutenant Colonel Sir,' I reported with a brittle voice. I had difficulty finding fitting words straight away. 'I can report the whole incident in detail to you. Herbert and I were close friends, and after being wounded he died in my arms.'

Unimaginably moving moments followed, and after Mr Niederländer had composed himself to some degree, he said to me: 'Let us find a room, my boy.' He pointed to the staff building of the barracks in which an office was made available to us.

Not once, no, two or three times I had to tell this story to the old gentleman so deeply affected by the death of his beloved son Herbert, who just as well might have been my father. Our conversation lasted several hours until evening. He did not want to let me go, and for him I served as kind of bridge into the afterlife to his dead son. Again and again Mr Niederländer questioned me about all the little details, and in the end he seemed grateful to me that he now had certainty about his son's death and together with his family could take his farewell in peace.

How many hundreds of thousands of missing soldiers might there have been in this war whose fate could never be resolved? They were all mourned, but haunting uncertainty pursued the relatives all their lives.

I did not believe my eyes when a few days later our grumpy sergeant major, with a growl, shoved a filled in leave pass for two weeks under my nose. This pass was signed by Lieutenant Colonel Niederländer. It was grotesque and macabre. I received two weeks' special leave as thanks for finally giving him certainty about the death of his lost son, leave for my friend Herbert who had died so young in my arms and was now lying buried far away in Russian soil.

Once again I quickly packed my belongings and as per regulations took my leave from our company commander, who had already been informed. Limping, I made it to the train station and travelled home whistling and in the best of moods via Saarbrücken, Trier, Wittlich and along the Moselle via Coblenz.

The two weeks on my family's farm were dominated by daily agricultural chores, which I once again carried out together with our Polish labourer. The days passed in a flash and after this additional time off I returned once more for another two and half months to Saarburg and my convalescent company.

At the end of autumn we were distributed among various marching groups according to our state of health. Due to my still restricted mobility I was not fit for the front and belonged to a group whose marching orders gave directions to a Wehrmacht barracks in the town of Thorn. So, together with some of my comrades, I went to the train station and travelled on completely overcrowded trains bursting with soldiers and civilians across our country now considerably marked by the war towards a new unknown destination with the interruption of several stopovers.

10

Transfer to Thorn at the Vistula

On this journey I could detect in many cities the terrible effects of the Allied bombing raids, which by day were flown by the US Army Air Force and by night by the British Royal Air Force. The damage was particularly bad in the Ruhr region.

Upon the arrival of our train at Düsseldorf Main Station the air-raid sirens rang out and sounded the pre-warning because of approaching bomber formations in the airspace of the Ruhr region. Along the platforms, voices, screams and commands echoed and boarding and alighting took place within three minutes. Immediately after, the locomotive pulled away and we left the endangered station under full steam toward Dortmund.

Our second-class compartment had been entered by a friendly and open Sturmbannführer of the Waffen-SS in black uniform, approximately fifteen years older, who sat down opposite me.

'Well, comrades, is your leave already over, too?' he cheerfully asked those present in the compartment. 'Surely we have a common destination: the Eastern Front!'

His casual manner and the callousness I had gained in active service caused me to face this man frankly. Rattled by rumours, tales, different opinions and reports about the deportations of the Jewish population, I spontaneously asked him the question that had been on my mind for a long time: 'Sturmbannführer Sir, can you tell me where the Jews have been deported?'

He answered directly and outright: 'The people were brought to various labour camps. It is known to me that a great number of them have also died there. I come, however, from the Waffen-SS and dissociate myself decidedly from the guard details of these camps, who also wear our SS uniform.'

Before I could ask him further questions, the train braked abruptly on the open track a few kilometres away from Dortmund. It was announced that the city was at that moment under attack by American bombers.

Due to the risk of strafers, we all left the train in a panic-stricken hurry and took cover at some distance from the railway embankment. From afar we watched the bombing of the city by endless heavy bomber formations.

Only when we heard the sirens in the distance give the all-clear in a long continuous tone, did we board the train again to continue our journey. I did not meet the Sturmbannführer again. Most likely he continued his travel in another compartment, and a little later the train slowly pulled up at the undamaged main station of Dortmund.

The bombing had been mainly directed at industrial complexes and some residential areas, which were blazing fiercely. The whole inferno gave all my travelling companions the creeps and everybody was glad when our train picked up speed again in order to leave the endangered Ruhr region as fast as possible. Via Berlin, where the damage was equally visible, and the following city of Poznan we reached our final destination, the town of Thorn on the Vistula, birthplace of Nicolaus Copernicus. This station, situated on the left bank of the Vistula, was teeming with bustling activity. I always had the impression that everyone was somehow looking for peace and quiet. We helped each other as far as possible, and the worse and more difficult the conditions became, the greater and closer the solidarity and team spirit of the people grew.

It seemed to me unbelievable, but it was true nevertheless! I could hardly believe my eyes when I recognised in the middle of the huge crowds of people a familiar face. Close to 20 million German soldiers were in this war on all fronts in Europe, and yet I discovered amidst the jostle of the totally overcrowded station of Thorn little Alfred Frensch from my home village Bassenheim, two years younger than me but now eighteen years old.

It was only a brief, but joyous encounter. Alfred was in a hurry, had little time and had to leave for his unit at the Eastern Front with the next train just pulling up. We could only exchange a few sentences, took our cordial farewells and wished each other luck. Would there be a reunion of us both at home one day?

Immediately after this encounter I marched, or rather limped, with another two comrades towards the barracks not far from the station that was listed in our marching orders. There we learned that we were intended as reinforcements for the guard details who had to monitor many thousands of prisoners of war held there. At first this seemed to us like a transfer for disciplinary reasons, but had the advantage that we did not have to return to the front that quickly.

The next day we saw the huge extent of the prisoner camp. For the most part Russian prisoners were accommodated here. To these were added some Italian soldiers who after Italy's changing of sides – until very recently allied with Germany – had also been detained here on short notice. Our task was not too difficult. In shifts I had to stand guard at the gate with some comrades and to let the prisoners out for work according to their allotted times and subsequently back in again.

The picture presenting itself here to me was harrowing. The general state of the imprisoned soldiers who passed by us looking miserable and starved was depressing. Every day dead people, mostly due to starvation, were carried from the camp. When of an evening these exhausted prisoners returned to the camp from their daily labour, which was continually monitored, we had to make sure that nothing unusual was smuggled into the camp. During this process we had to search the trouser pockets of these people, among other things.

After initial spot checks on the poor creatures of the same age as me it soon became clear to me and my comrades that there was absolutely nothing to find. All we discovered were perhaps a couple of old, half-rotten potatoes or edible bits that had occasionally been slipped to the poor devils by a compassionate soul.

It would never have entered my mind to take something from these people, least of all food. On the contrary! As often as the occasion presented itself to me, I slipped the prisoners leftovers of bread or other food during my duty. This took place during their leaving in the morning or their return in the evening. This was, of course, not without risk and had to take place unobtrusively. Nationality was of no matter to me here. Although I slipped that which I could rustle up mostly to the emaciated Russian soldiers, a detained Italian fighter pilot of my age who was not assigned to any work had also caught my eye. He showed himself particularly grateful for an additional piece of bread.

Whenever the occasion arose I listened to Mario when, in broken German, he spoke of his experiences as a fighter pilot. We became friends, and as thanks he gave me his address and invited me to visit him and his family in Turin after the war. According to his telling, his parents owned a large factory there and were very wealthy. He wanted to show his gratitude for my help by any means. After a few weeks' internment in the camp Mario was released.

One evening I witnessed an incident that occurred when for a change I stood guard at the gate with Corporal Hoffmann. By now I recognised many of their faces and knew who smuggled something edible into the camp if the occasion arose. On this evening Hoffmann discovered some old, half-rotten potatoes in the trouser pockets of two Russian prisoners, from which the poor lads had wanted to make a little additional meal for themselves.

'Come on, you thieves, turn out and empty all your pockets,' Hoffmann yelled at the two emaciated creatures. 'You know very well that it is a punishable offence to smuggle food or other items into the camp.'

Without another word he took the shabby potatoes from them. I found the behaviour of our corporal so deplorable that this incident depressed me for days.

From then on I made an increased effort to distribute alms, whenever it was possible for me, knowing very well that there was some risk to me in it and that it was no more than a drop in the ocean in view of the mass of prisoners. It gave me some satisfaction, and several other comrades did the same.

The misery of the prisoner of war camp was a sad accompaniment to this war. If the manageable number of prisoners from the campaigns in Poland and France were still allocated throughout the Reich as assistants in agriculture and armament production, so the mass of Russian soldiers was detained in camps. Accommodation, food and medical treatment were extremely inadequate, and countless numbers of them died in the camps – mostly of starvation. A sad, shameful and inhumane tally!

These were the conditions – or even worse – that must have been suffered by the more than 90,000 German prisoners of war from the Stalingrad pocket, and this under adverse climatic conditions. After many years of imprisonment only 6,000 of these men returned, aged decades and marked by suffering. To these were added further hundreds of thousands of men who had to do forced labour in Russian labour camps and mines. Of these an unimaginable number died, too. The last almost 10,000 German soldiers only returned in 1955, after the then Chancellor Konrad Adenauer had secured their release through tough bargaining with Moscow.

Violations of the Geneva Convention occurred by all states involved in the war, even the democratic western powers. As a rule German PoWs were treated humanely and fairly in the United States, Canada or Britain, but after the mass capitulations in the final phase of the war thousands of them had to live out in the open in the Allied camps on the Rhine meadows at Sinzig, Remagen, Andernach, Mainz-Bretzenheim or Frankfurt at the Main. Many of them died of dehydration and starvation. As a rule the victims were always the simple soldiers, less the high-ranking officers.

Once again, I did not spend my twentieth birthday and Christmas 1943 at home, but at the Thorn camp. The holidays, which were not festive at all either for us or for the prisoners, were spent in an unspectacular and depressing way at the camp.

Shortly before Christmas I received a small package from Mother. This was filled with a small cured sausage, a dry cake and a letter with news from our home. Therein she wrote:

Dear Fritz,

How are you? I hope you are well out at the front and that you are in good health. Do you have enough to eat? Your brothers Hans and Peter are still stationed in France. Hans is near Paris, and Peter is located at the French Channel Coast. About Karl's whereabouts I cannot tell you anything unfortunately. Of your uncle Peter Paul, the second boy, your cousin Georg, has fallen in Russia. I am so worried about you, Fritz, and hope that I will see you again safe and sound. From our Bassenheim castle Senior Lieutenant Helmut Friedrich Julius Richard Count von Waldhausen has likewise fallen in Russia. The two daughters Ellionor and Bettina are only one and three years old. The entire village expressed great sympathy for Helmut's death, as the von Waldhausen family held close ties to our village and community and always made an effort to contribute to the common good of the population and the whole parish.

Unfortunately I further have to tell you that a second close friend of your childhood and youth, Arnold Lohner, has fallen. He went down with a navy ship and drowned.

Life at home becomes more difficult from week to week. The food stamps are few and have to be used carefully for food, shoes, and clothes. Luckily the supply of staples still works quite well for us farmers. Yet the lack of sugar is very inconvenient. I wish you, my beloved boy, luck a thousand times and I pray every evening and every morning for you and your brothers, that we may all see each other again safe and sound and in peace, God willing. Take care of yourself, my Fritz!

Your mother, loving you with all her heart.

This package was the last mail I received during the war. From then on none of us brothers knew how each other and the rest of the family were faring.

There was no longer any good news at that time and no reason for joy. Among the few comforts was the one Sunday off a month. Then we went as a group of some comrades on foot across the wide Vistula bridge in order to explore the very beautiful, wealthy historic district of Thorn. We learned much about the town's history and visited some of the lovely street cafés. Here there were magnificent residences steeped in history, administrative buildings and churches. The splendour and wealth of the gorgeous historical town were impressive.

In spring 1944 the military situation in the Wehrmacht deteriorated further and further; the Eastern Front moved inexorably towards the west, the southern front in Italy towards the north, the aerial raids on our cities increased in intensity, the invasion of the Allied armed forces in the west was in the offing, and the last reserves were mobilised in Germany.

Armament production achieved record numbers, and the last human reserves were mobilised to reinforce the front and to furnish it with weapons. Also drafted into the fighting units were Hitler Youth members, old men of the Volkssturm, established in autumn 1944, and most of all convalescing wounded soldiers who could just about walk and shoot.

In the meantime our camp had been so decimated in numbers due to death among the prisoners that it was closed. The survivors were transferred to another camp.

What this meant for us who were just about fit for duty within limits could be easily guessed. After a brief medical examination we received the stamp 'KV' (*kriegsverwendungsfähig* = fit for active service) in our identification and service book, which meant my second deployment to the front.

11

With the Tank Assault Regiment to the Eastern Front

Together with some of my comrades, I was assigned to Tank Assault Regiment PAOK 4, which was hastily established in May 1944. The regiment had been formed from the training battalion of the Army Weapons Schools and put under the control of the 4th Tank Army. It was divided into two battalions with four companies each. Here we received a brief training in the new close-combat weapons, the Panzerfaust and the Panzerschrek, both anti-tank rocket launchers. These were increasingly used in courageous close-combat missions on the front line against the overwhelming superiority of the Allies in tanks.

Having just been promoted to lance corporal, after less than three weeks training I was transferred by train with this unit to Army Group Centre for the reinforcement of the 4th Tank Army deployed there. Having arrived at the front line, we were immediately thrown into the intense defensive battles that were raging.

This was a motley crew of experienced veteran squaddies, some already wounded several times, volunteers from the Hitler Youth, very few elderly Volkssturm soldiers, soldiers from the Luftwaffe, navy and artillery who no longer had any aircraft, ships and cannons, and staff duty soldiers of wiped out units, who were fighting at the front line for the first time.

Nobody knew the other, and everyone was a stranger to everybody else. Here comradeships forged over weeks and months no longer existed. For many nothing mattered but themselves, and surviving at any cost became the top priority. We were not the last resort by any means, but we were a colourful bunch, deployed to save the western world from Bolshevism and facing an overpowering, rapidly advancing enemy. Luckily the injury to my emaciated left leg had healed to the extent that I was only limping very slightly. Even running was somewhat manageable, but nothing much remained of my former good acceleration.

I experienced my first mission in the defence of our section, through which a road ran and led across an old stone bridge that crossed a wider brook. The course of the brook was cut into the ground deeply like a wedge and thus had the effect of a natural, insurmountable anti-tank ditch. Whoever wanted to break through here had try to get across the bridge. The structure had a bottleneck effect and according to our orders was not to be blown up but turned into a trap for the Russian tank spearheads.

For this purpose two marksmen were posted left and right of the bridge's abutment on our side, dug into their positions, which were well hidden and camouflaged. These were courageous young soldiers who had volunteered for this task. One of them was equipped with a Panzerfaust, the other with an equally new Panzerschrek. The order was: 'Let the first tank through and destroy the second in the middle of the bridge.' As a consequence a tailback was to be caused and hence a further advance of the enemy tanks delayed because of the blockage caused. The fight against the further accruing and halting Soviet tanks was to be carried out by us with our anti-tank handheld weapons and concentrated charges, depending on the situation.

My arms consisted of a Schmeisser MP 40 machine pistol and a con-centrated charge made from three stick grenades bound together. In the provisionally dug rear trench we observed with our unit the deployment of the Russian offensive. The thrumming of the tank engines rose to a mighty pitch. Inside me suddenly rose again the same feeling of trepidation as two years ago at the Volkhov front near Leningrad, when the Russian tank assault could be repelled at the last moment by our 88mm cannons. Here at this spot there were hardly any cannons left that could have come to our aid and protect us. Here we were on our own.

The attack of the superior Soviet army proceeded sure-footedly and with the vigour of the certain victor. The first tank passed cautiously over the bridge and our whole unit remained undiscovered. When the second tank drove across the centre of the bridge, our two comrades fired their two armour-piercing weapons. It was a fiasco without end! Both projectiles missed their target, the enemy was forewarned, and one tank after another now rushed forward at high speed. For us there was no chance to actually fight the fast, dangerous T-34s and no holding back. Without heavy weap-onry we were virtually helpless. The remaining Panzerfaust were fired with little success, and the whole unit retreated as quickly as possible. Apart from a few shot-down Russian tanks and some comrades who had been rolled over and squashed into a bloody pulp by the monsters, this attack did not have any serious consequences.

This was followed again day in and day out by a desperate holding of the front with the modest personal and material means available to us. After five years of war, Germany, its people and especially the soldiers at the front felt the looming defeat and impending downfall approaching from all sides.

In June 1944 the German Army Group Centre under General Field Marshal Ernst Busch had only about forty divisions with around 500,000 men left. Time and again, however, Adolf Hitler rejected the urgent demands by Wehrmacht command to move back a 1,000-kilometre long arch of the front formed by Army Group Centre far into the east around Vitebsk, Orsha, Mogilev and Bobruisk. Two weeks after the opening of a new front in the west by the invasion of the Western Allies of Normandy, on 22 June 1944 the Red Army began a large-scale offensive against Army Group Centre. The German Luftwaffe could confront the roughly 6,000 Russian aircraft with only forty of their own.

After their breach of the front, 1.2 million Soviet soldiers with 4,000 tanks commenced a pincer movement between Vitebsk and Bobruisk, which led to the encirclement of the German 4th and 9th Armies as well as the 3rd Tank Army. Within a few days the enemy had advanced 300 kilometres into the west. On 3 July Minsk was liberated, ten days later Vilnius. When Busch's successor General Field Marshal Walter Model stopped the advance for a short while at the end of July along the line Kovno–Brest-Litovsk, the Army Group Centre had effectively ceased to exist.

The collapse of Army Group Centre was more dramatic for the Wehrmacht than the battle of Stalingrad. From this blow the entire eastern army could never recover again. In late summer of 1944 the front reached East Prussia's borders. The Soviet front lines inserted themselves between the Army Groups Centre and North and the Wehrmacht lost its operational flexibility.

Around 350,000 German soldiers had fallen or been taken prisoner by the Soviets within only four weeks. On many of these days filled with heavy losses, 10,000 soldiers died per day, just as they had with us at the Eastern Front – an unimaginably high and horrible number of young people who lost their lives only shortly after finishing school or their apprenticeship. After the crushing defeat the Red Army streamed through a 400-kilometre gap towards East Prussia and Warsaw. On 24 July the 1st Belarusian Front conquered Lublin. One day earlier they had managed to liberate the extermination camp Majdanek, before the crematoria, gas chambers and other evidence of the National Socialist mass extermination could be destroyed.

The liberation of the concentration camps and the inhuman conditions found there stoked the hatred of the Soviet soldiers against us, the so-called 'Germanic master race'. 'They sow the wind and reap the whirlwind' was a German proverb. We not only reaped whirlwinds, but hurricanes of cruelties. Now we felt the effects of Hitler's inhumane policies against other peoples in their most terrible form. In many announcements and millions of leaflets, the Russian author Ilya Grigoryevich Ehrenburg now incited like a mantra Russian soldiers to unrestrained mass murder of the German population in return.

No other Russian name apart from Stalin caused a comparable terror in Germans of the war generation than that of Ilya Ehrenburg. Contemporary witnesses and historiography agree that his leaflets and articles with statements such as: 'Kill! The Germans are no humans!' which were regularly published in the party newspaper *Pravda* and the front newspaper *Krasnaya Svesda*, substantially prepared and triggered the excesses of the Red Army in East Germany.

Here are a few examples, which I do not wish to hold back and which describe unmistakably how the countless and horrid excesses against the German civilian population could come about:

'Our business is to kill Germans, it does not matter how.'
'If you have killed a German, then kill a second, for us there is nothing funnier than German corpses.'
'If you are a just and conscientious person, kill a German.'
'The German must be killed. One has to kill him.'
'If you feel bad, kill a German.'
'Just count one thing, the Germans killed by you.'
'The best Germans are dead Germans.'
'The problem is whether it is better to slay the Germans with axes or with cudgels.'

All these terrible appeals and the atrocities of the Red Army resulting from them were known to me and all other squaddies. They were, of course, exploited by our own propaganda and spread among the troops like wildfire. Everybody knew that it was too late to turn the tide of war once more, but with calls for perseverance all soldiers were to be motivated to keep the enemy away from Germany's borders as long as possible. By invoking the upcoming deployment of wonder weapons, courage was stoked where everything was already lost. We saw the tragedy with our own eyes, the suffering and the murder of the German population in the east. Besides Hitler's categorical order to hold out it was certainly also this gruesome scenario that contributed to keeping the battle-weary and decimated eastern army together. For we tried in good faith to save what could no longer be saved.

The Russian offensive on Warsaw at the end of July came to a halt 25 kilometres outside the city. Stalin had no interest whatsoever in the success of the ongoing Jewish and national Polish uprising. Rather he was keen to install the Communist Lublin Committee as Poland's compliant government after the conquest of the capital. Therefore he ordered his armies to idly stand by and watch the German suppression of the uprising.

In the north the 1st Baltic Front cut off Army Group North from all overland links to East Prussia, after they had pushed forward into the gap between Army Groups Centre and North south of Dinaburg and had reached the Bay of Riga at the end of July 1944.

Until mid-October, Army Group North retreated to Courland, where they later held their ground in costly battles until the German capitulation on 8 May 1945. Among the units to perish there was my former 132nd Infantry Division.

As the Red Army suffered in part from considerable supply problems due to their rapid advance in autumn 1944, the Eastern Front was stabilised until the Soviet winter offensive of 1945. A Soviet offensive on East Prussian Königsberg initiated in mid-October could be repelled by German troops until the beginning of November, but in south-eastern Europe the Soviet advance progressed inexorably with the conquest of the entire Balkan region. The occupation of Romania and Bulgaria as well as of Hungarian territories from October 1944 made the evacuation of Wehrmacht-occupied Greece necessary. Army Group E retreated a little later to allied Croatia via Albania and Serbia.

The daily defensive skirmishes until far into autumn 1944 meant that the fight for survival became ever more difficult and full of privation. There was no longer any thought of regular food, body care and hygiene for weeks, even months. Medical treatment was only available within limits or not at all. Clothing and equipment were restricted to that which we carried on our bodies. In almost all areas we had to take care of our daily needs on our own. Lack of food and sleep, in addition to the cold of the severe winter of 1944/45, drained us army soldiers. Every night we holed up somewhere else. Sometimes this was in a stable, in barns, in forests, in hedges or out in the open in any kind of hole in the ground. To this were added costly rearguard actions and the manifold terror of death.

The units flowing back were gathered over and over in new provisional reception positions and restructured. Yet the enemy stormed against our lines with a monstrous superiority of people and material, with thousands of tanks, ordnance, ground attack aircraft, fighter planes and bombers. We, on the other hand, were plagued by hunger. Everywhere there was a lack of weapons and ammunition. Every bullet was counted out. A turn in the fate of war was totally unlikely in spite of calls for perseverance and courage and propagandistic appeals.

I faced the same terrifying situation again and again. Once again an assault by the Russians after their usual massive artillery preparation from countless guns was imminent. From the intensity and number of shots, we experienced front soldiers surmised an enormous concentration of enemy artillery. It was a virtual inferno that came over us.

We sought out any kind of depression in the ground for cover and as protection against the explosive effects of mortars and shrapnel. My cover was flimsy, and so I attempted a change in position and landed mid–jump in a large shell crater that was already fully occupied by squaddies seeking shelter. An old soldier's rule is that where once a mortar has hit no second will hit again. Eight to ten men were crouching tightly pressed together in this large hole. These shouted and ranted in their panic that there was no space left and that I should kindly bugger off, and indeed the crater would have offered only slightly improved cover.

With a few strides I jumped into a smaller shell crater circa eight to ten metres away and pressed my face onto the cold soil. The air was heavy with acrid gun smoke, and with every close impact I had the feeling of being lifted into the air by several centimetres just to land back on the ground. When a high-calibre mortar detonated only a few metres away from my cover, I secretly resigned myself to die.

Yet the projectile had not hit my shell crater, but had hit the neighbouring crater filled with the many squaddies, out of which I had just jumped. Upon me and my uniform and scattered all around me lay torn, bloody limbs, heads, brain tissue and intestines. It was grisly! Nobody heard my screams of shock or saw my blood-smeared uniform. The thunderous battle noise drowned everything out, and I was trembling in my whole body.

None of these soldiers had survived the impact. All had been torn and shredded apart. My life had once again hung by a thread. Had it simply been soldier's luck again for the umpteenth time or had our Lord held his sheltering hand over me? In situations like this panic grips a person, you are no longer able to hold a clear thought and are acting only out of experience and instinct.

The enemy was battering us ever more severely with his immense superiority and forced our units into a hasty retreat. The day after the next we were attacked from the air. Numerous Russian Il-2 ground attack planes were on the approach and fired at our provisional weak positions, from which we had to rapidly retreat again. All who were able to run ran towards the west, but the aircraft created total confusion.

I ran and jumped as best I could, from one cover to the next. Suddenly I saw a ground attack plane approaching me directly after a narrow turn. Without thinking of my damaged leg, I ran for my life and threw myself in a full-length dive behind a metre-thick tree. The projectile volleys hit this tree and the ground all around it. When the aircraft was passing, I could clearly make out the face of this Russian pilot. Apparently he had solely aimed for me.

When he turned for a second time and approached me in order to kill me, my only chance was to run to the other side of the thick tree and to hope that the aircraft was no longer carrying any bombs. Once again part of the projectiles hailed down on the tree, and additional ones hit the ground a few centimetres away from me. Yet the feared impact of a bomb never happened. The aircraft turned away. The shadowy face of the Russian pilot looking at me haunted me over and over again in my dreams of later years, and I have never forgotten it.

Once more our greatly decimated troops were assigned to new reserve units. These consisted in part of small tank units that were equipped with the then most modern and powerful tanks of the world. Among these were types such as the Tiger, Jagdtiger and Tiger II, also the Panther and Jagdpanther. I very clearly recall a tank unit of at least thirty-five Tigers, assault guns and armoured reconnaissance cars as leading vehicles. While we marched back to a new cushioning line, these very young, fearless tank soldiers on their fatal drive tore towards the front and the enemy in the east for the first time. Full of euphoria, confidence in victory and courage, they called to us during a brief stop at the same spot: 'Have no fear, we will stop the enemy, no Russian shall pass us!'

These poor boys, I thought. A cruel death will befall them all in no time. They will explode, be torn apart or burn most gruesomely. They might be sitting inside top products of German military technology, of which one was worth five enemy tanks, but they could never cope with such superiority. In spite of their unmatched armoured protection and the most powerful tank cannons, they were sitting in travelling coffins and driving towards certain death. Did it matter in the end, though, whether death found a person in the then best tank in the world or in a trench by a bullet or grenade?

Although I was close to my twenty-first birthday during these apocalyptic weeks, I felt ancient compared to those seventeen- and eighteen-year-old tank soldiers. I did not only feel like it, but looked like an old man, too: emaciated, grey, dirty, unshaven and unwashed for weeks. Nothing remained in these days of the former proud, fit, dashing, straight young Wehrmacht soldier rude of health. How miserable must we and the remains of our once glorious and victorious army have seemed to the young tank soldiers!

When we passed a lonely Polish farm, I became aware that I had hardly eaten anything for days and weeks. Hunger was torturing me. The poor Polish farmers peered out fearfully from behind the curtains of a window. I felt pity for them, and I was too embarrassed to enter their house with a loaded MP to ask for something to eat. I slung my MP across my back, ran to the chicken coop, caught the first chicken crossing my path, wrung its neck and stuffed the dead animal into my field bag. Hunger drove me to this deed. I was already fantasizing about a juicy roast, which I intended to prepare shortly on a camp fire for my enjoyment.

During our rapid withdrawal from the enemy I plucked the creature during our next halt and put it back into the bag. The pressure by the following Red Army was so immense, however, that there were no more halts and most of all no opportunity to gut the chicken and to somehow cook or roast it. It kept quite well in the extreme cold, but after three days I had to throw it away. I could not still my hunger and scoffed down a hard bread crust and a tiny piece of bacon.

Compared to the many dead and the many cruelties we experienced and had to suffer daily, the senseless theft of the chicken from the Polish family depressed me for a long time, strangely enough. I felt sorry, and I could not forgive myself for years for stealing that chicken without asking the people. Only a few days later a similar situation presented itself during our hurried retreat. With five soldiers out of my company, which now only consisted of eighteen men, I decided late in the evening, being completely frozen in the darkness, to stay the night on a large Polish farm.

'I am asking for a place to sleep for me and my comrades and for something to eat,' said the comrade who had entered first with a trembling voice to the fearful inhabitants of the farm. 'We are all terribly hungry and have eaten almost nothing for days.' Apart from a large number of eggs, some bacon, dried meat, beans and dry bread, these people had not much more to eat themselves during this bitter last winter of the war. They rustled up all kinds of stuff, however, to somehow feed us pathetic-looking, emaciated, miserable creatures. We must have presented a wretched picture. Our hosts told us that they themselves were in fear of the approaching front and the Russian soldiers. We were all allowed to sit down together with the farmer's family around a large wooden table in the warm kitchen heated by a tiled stove in order to eat our late night meal.

In spite of the relatively abundant offer of food, my stomach could not accept any larger amount. In contrast to me and four other comrades, who likewise filled their weaned stomachs moderately and carefully, the sixth squaddie became out of his senses with greed and began a virtual eating orgy. Against our warnings, he stuffed bread, bacon, cheese and twelve eggs into his emaciated body.

We were allowed to sleep in the straw of the barn. As we were no longer cold and were well sated, this could have been the most pleasant night for a long while if there had not been the dull rumble and thunder of the approaching front.

In the darkness of the winter morning we hastily set off towards the west – yet now there was only five of us. Our sixth comrade, who had eaten more than triple our late-night meal, had died quietly during the night without us noticing. He had probably been so weakened and emaciated that the excessive amount of food led to his death. Due to our necessary haste we did not even have enough time to dig a grave for him.

Days later we passed a recently vacated jam factory, probably abandoned in panic. Constantly in search of something to eat, I stole three buckets of jam from the stores. After a short while the buckets' metal straps cut so painfully into my frozen hands in the icy cold that I exchanged two buckets of jam for a loaf of bread with a squaddie crossing our path. We ate, no, we all greedily devoured as much bread and jam as possible. We had not known sweet jam for many months.

When the comrade donating the bread briefly took off his coat, I recognised a grenadier officer in a major's uniform. He was caught in the maelstrom of the fleeing Wehrmacht, too, and thoroughly enjoyed the fruity delicacy amidst the circle of us comrades. In those days ranks no longer played any great role. Everybody tried to somehow survive this downfall.

The military situation in late autumn 1944 was the following: in the west the Wehrmacht retreated until September 1944 back to the former Reich borders with an increasing lack of personnel and material after the Allied Operation Overlord. At the Eastern Front it found itself in a precarious situation after the Soviet summer offensives, in whose course it had to accept the so far most bitter defeats in this war along a front of 2,500 kilometres. After the collapse of Army Group Centre in the course of Operation Bagration during June and July, Army Group Northern Ukraine was resoundingly defeated in July and August during the Lvov-Sandomierz Offensive, and shortly after Army Group Southern Ukraine was virtually destroyed in the Jassy-Kishinev Offensive.

Army Group North, which at the beginning of September had still been able to hold Estonia, western Latvia and a narrow land bridge to Army Group Centre, was cut off with twenty-seven divisions after the breakthrough of Soviet units to the Baltic Sea in the context of the Baltic operations in October.

In the north the German troops had to be pulled back from northern Norway after Finland signed the armistice of Moscow with the Soviet Union on 4 September 1944.

In the southern part of the Eastern Front the gate to the Balkans was opened for the Soviet Union after Romania's switch to the Allies (by a coup d'état on 23 August 1944). The Soviet Union declared war on Bulgaria on 5 September. Soviet tanks reached the Romanian–Yugoslavian border at the beginning of September, advanced by mid-September into the Hungarian lowlands and on 29 October began the battle of Budapest. Counter-attacks by the Wehrmacht managed to stabilise the Eastern Front temporarily towards the end of November along a length of 1,200 kilometres between the Baltic Sea and the Carpathian Mountains.

From July until November 1944 all three army groups (North, Centre, and South) of the eastern army had lost around 1.2 million soldiers. In November, 131 German divisions, of which thirty-two were tied down in Courland (among them my 132nd Infantry Division) and seventeen in Hungary, were standing opposite roughly 225 infantry divisions and about fifty major tank units of the Red Army. In the south-east the Russian successes during the Belgrade operation put the German occupying forces in Greece, Albania and Yugoslavia at risk of being cut off.

The retreat of Army Group E signalled at the beginning of October proceeded in an orderly way at first, but by November it became ever more difficult to hold the front between Drava near the Adriatic and Lake Balaton, after a connection had been made with Army Group South. The Italian theatre of war had lost considerable importance after the Allied invasion of Normandy. At the end of November, Army Group C could hold the line La Spezia–Rimini across the Apennines with twenty-three divisions of varying quality. Nevertheless, the entanglement of these forces by the Allies and by lively partisan activity carried weight in the whole.

On the western front the Allies had taken over the initiative through their victories near Avranches and Falaise. In extremely costly battles, Army Group B (General Field Marshal Model) retreated across the Seine towards the east. A noticeable difference to the Eastern Front lay in the fact that the German losses in the west were at least as high as those of the Allies.

After the landing of American and French troops near Toulon on 15 August (Operation Dragon), the two remaining German armies of Army Group B at the Atlantic Ocean (Bordeaux) and the Mediterranean Sea had to be pulled back; the attackers advanced rapidly through the Rhône valley.

At the beginning of September the retreat of the western army came to a halt along a line that led from the mouth of the Scheldt in southern Holland to the Siegfried Line south of Trier, from there followed the Moselle and then reached the Swiss border. All German units were severely battered, thinned out and hardly in possession of heavy weaponry. A chronic lack of fuel led to a loss of mobility, which had a particularly serious effect due to the Allies' air superiority.

The Siegfried Line was hastily rebuilt and occupied with rapidly mustered units. In mid-September, with Army Group B (mouth of the Scheldt to Trier) along a front length of 400 kilometres, twenty-one infantry divisions and seven tank divisions faced far superior Allied forces. By late autumn

1944 the Wehrmacht had been pushed back to the former Reich territory on all fronts. On 21 October Aachen was first German city conquered by the Allies. These showed themselves superior in men and material with an increasing tendency and used this potential in order to take the operational initiative.

There was no thought of changing these circumstances from a German point of view. On the contrary: the maritime war, which on the German side could now only be fought as submarine warfare against enemy trade and transport ships, had been lost since 1943. From the beginning of that year the increase of tonnage surpassed the losses of the Allies. Equally, the aerial war had been long since decided in 1944. Along the front and above Reich territory, the Allies had absolute air supremacy.

In substantial ignorance of foreign policy relationships, Hitler came to the conclusion that the coalition of his adversaries was near to failure. He was therein inspired by his role model Friedrich II of Prussia, who through the sudden death of the Russian Tzarina Elisabeth had been saved from a hopeless military situation. He hoped that it would only require a painful blow against the western Allies, whose combat strength he assessed as less than that of the Red Army, and then the alliance between the western powers and the USSR, unnatural in his eyes, would shatter. The Anglo-Americans would retreat to their home countries, and the German Reich would be able to successfully end its defensive battle in the east against the threatening Bolshevisation of Europe. Such a shock to the political balance could, in Hitler's opinion, only be achieved by a decisive military success at the western front. For this he was ready to stake his last reserves. According to his Darwinist world view, the German people had to win or, if it was not able to do so, to perish.

In no other operation of the war did Hitler's irrational wishful thinking became more apparent; never was the chasm between delusion and reality greater.

12

The Downfall in Sight

At the turn of the year 1944/45, with our severely decimated companies, we could just about escape over the Vistula. Here we were integrated into one of the last retaining lines, which consisted of all kinds of troop elements flooding back and newly established Volkssturm and Hitler Youth groups in their hundreds. It was the very last resort of the stricken Wehrmacht. We were no longer dashing soldiers, but an ultimately betrayed generation ground down for years, drained, and wounded in body and soul.

In spite of all the suffering, the principle of order and obedience still worked as well as the Prussian virtues, especially that of comradeship. We were no wild mercenary troop who marauded across the land. No, we were still the somehow functioning Wehrmacht, which now defended our own country as effectively as possible in a hopeless battle and tried to protect the population.

My twenty-first birthday and Christmas following two days later were cancelled. There were neither presents nor culinary delights, but just the painful, uncertain thoughts of home and of my family. We were homesick and longed for peace. I had spent the previous two birthdays and Christmas holidays away from home, and they had not been jolly. Yet this time sheer desperation overcame us. Freezing, strained and hungry, we were constructing trenches, positions and earth bunkers as protection against the expected enemy attacks.

In the west the Americans had already crossed the Reich's borders in several places and were standing deep on German ground. In the south, in Italy, the Anglo-American troops advanced towards the north. Upon the seven seas almost all German capital ships had been destroyed. Only a few had been able to escape to the Baltic Sea, where they were now needed for transporting refugees along the Baltic Sea coast. These ships meant for many people from East and West Prussia and Pomerania, for whom the escape cross-country had been cut off, their last hope of escape to the west. The initially so successful submarines, the 'grey wolves', were sunk by the dozens thanks to the new detection devices of the Allies and they suffered the highest losses of all the military branches. Of 40,000 submarine operators, 30,000 did not return.

Most of the larger German cities were razed to the ground under a hailstorm of bombs without the German Luftwaffe being able to put up any resistance worth mentioning. The German aviation industry developed types with far superior flight performance such as the jet Messerschmitt Me 262 or the Heinkel He 162 Salamander, also called the People's Fighter, or rocket-powered fighters such as the Messerschmitt Me 163 and the Bachem Natter, but their small numbers and the lack of trained pilots and fuel prevented their effective use.

While the bombing war caused ever more terrible casualties among the civilian population, Nazi propaganda boasted about the devastating effect of their 'wonder weapons' and tried to motivate the nation to hold out with snappy words about final victory. Indeed, the inventions of the winged bomb V1 and the rocket V 2 were ground-breaking. These weapons wrung some respect from the Allies and caused terror in London, the preferred target. If the rockets reached their target, they caused considerable destruction and claimed many victims.

In comparison to the heavy bombing raids in Germany, the German attacks were more like pinpricks, and the British losses of 60,000 civilians were only a tenth of the German casualties. However, the intended effect of breaking the morale of the civilian population was not achieved either by the Germans or the Allies.

At the beginning of the last year of war the situation for the German Wehrmacht, especially for us in the east, was extremely tense, but relatively stable. After the conclusion of the Soviet summer offensives that reached the Vistula, and after the termination of combat in East Prussia in October 1944, the fronts in East Prussia and Poland remained essentially unchanged until January 1945. Yet every day we had to reckon with a new offensive by the Soviets. Nevertheless, several German divisions were pulled out from East Prussia and the Vistula front in winter 1944/45 and in part transferred to Hungary, in part to the Rhine front where on 16 December the German Ardennes Offensive began. Thus the forces available at the Eastern Front had been further weakened. Behind the thinly manned front line hardly any reserves fit for combat still existed that could have been deployed in case of a potential breakthrough of Soviet troops.

At the beginning of January, the German command knew of the concentration of Russian forces more than ten times superior, in particular in the region of the three Russian bridgeheads over the Vistula, Baranów, Pulawy and Magnuszew, in whose area our units were situated. In spite of urgent presentations to the Führer's headquarters, no reinforcements could be made available, let alone be transferred. Thereby it became clear that the expected Russian large-scale offensive must entail a military disaster and carry off the civilian population in its maelstrom.

If the fierce battles in all theatres of war of the Second World War had made a precautionary evacuation of the civilian population necessary if possible and had caused refugee movements everywhere, the dire experiences of the first incursions of Russian troops onto German soil in East Prussia incited virtual panic. The only chance for the civilian population lay in evading the grasp of the Red Army by timely flight. If and to what extent there were still opportunities to escape would entirely depend on the rapidity and direction of the Russian offensives, which were very different in the various areas of operation. The military operations determined to a large extent escape routes, direction of escape and the origin of certain focal points in refugee movement.

From 12 to 15 January the long-planned Russian large-scale offensive took place with the individual thrusts from the various deployment areas being staggered in short intervals along the entire front from the Neman River in the north to the Upper Vistula in the south.

The remaining German troops with a strength of 569,000 men, 8,230 pieces of ordnance, 700 tanks and 1,300 aircraft (approximately the same number of forces were at the same time being used in the Ardennes Offensive against US troops in the west) were faced by a superior Russian force of 1.5 million soldiers, 28,000 pieces of ordnance, 3,300 tanks and 10,000 aircraft.

For the Red Army this was the final tremendous exertion of force in the Second World War. In order to boost its men's will to fight, once again millions of leaflets were distributed, calling on the destruction of the 'Fascist animal' in its den and the rape of the 'Germanic women'. The hour of death had been tolled for the German population in the east.

First the troops of the 1st Ukrainian Front (General Konjev) broke out of the Baranów bridgehead towards Silesia on 12 January, then on the 13th followed the attack of the 1st Belarusian Front (General Shukov) from the Vistula bridgeheads Magnuszew and Pulawy, which was set up for a frontal advance via Lodz and Kalisz towards the middle Oder.

Two further thrusts were to cut off East Prussia: on 13 January the attack of the 3rd Belarusian Front (Tchernajkovsky) from the east toward Königsberg took place first, while two days later on 15 January followed a thrust set up from the Narew bridgehead Pultusk via Chiechanow and Szkotowo by the 2nd Belarusian Front (Rokossovsky), which aimed at Thorn and Elbing in order to cut off East Prussia from the German Reich.

The Soviet attacks, carried out with an enormous deployment of troops and materiel, achieved great successes after a few days. The situation on the German defensive front became worst in the large Vistula bulge, where we were lying with our units of the 4th Army Corps, and also in the Warsaw region. Along the entire front line there was practically no holding back any more against this vast firestorm of the Red Army.

On the first day the latter achieved deep breakthroughs, and on 15 January no cohesive German front remained in this region. In the southern part of the Vistula front, breakthroughs and bypasses could only be prevented by the fact that the German troops were retreating to the west before the superior Soviet armed forces, at least maintaining the cohesion of the front.

With the enemy on our tail pressing us relentlessly with full force, we sometimes covered 40 to 50 kilometres per day through the deeply snowed in countryside. On 18 January Shukov's and Konjev's armies were situated along the line Plock–Lodz–Czestochowa–Cracow while still advancing rapidly. Between them some German units were still on the move, trying to break through to the west.

On 20 January Russian troops crossed the old Reich border east of Wroclaw and advanced to the outer areas of the Upper Silesian industrial region. A few days later they reached the Oder near Brzeg (23 January) and north of Wroclaw near Ścinawa (28 January).

In the Warthegau (the annexed Polish province of Poznan) the towns of Wrzesnia and Gniezno were occupied by Russian troops at that time. On 25 January they had encircled Poznan Fortress, which capitulated on 23 February. And still Shukov's troops pressed forth farther to the west in rapid advance. Their spearheads soon thrust on both sides past the Obra position and during the last days of January they reached the Oder near Fürstenberg and Küstrin. On 2/3 February all of East Brandenburg was occupied by Russian troops.

In the shortest time the Soviet assault armies had advanced from the great Vistula bulge to the middle reaches of the Oder and together with the German troops had also driven the German population fleeing from Warthegau and East Brandenburg before them. As a result of the rapidity of the Russian advance, many refugee trails had been overtaken on their way to the west. Only those who had crossed the Oder in time were safe for now, because the front came to a halt until April along the middle reaches of the Oder.

During the retreat of our troops, civilians on numerous refugee trails who were looking for protection and help mingled with our Wehrmacht units time and again. Entire village communities fled towards the west in blind panic in their horse carts but for a large part on foot.

Much too late, the respective regional leaderships had begun to evacuate the civilian population from East and West Prussia, and from Pomerania and Silesia. Hundreds of thousands of people were fleeing, partly together with us retreating troops. The harrowing drama took its course. Millions of old men, women, children and babies were on these refugee trails, among them numerous little children who had lost their parents to death or separation in the turmoil of war and who did not even knew their own names, let alone where they should go.

Many of the old people, children and particularly babies did not survive the hardships. There were hardly any warm meals, no milk, no baby food, no medicine, no warmth and hardly any shelter. Due to the haste necessary and the bitterly cold, sustained winter weather with extreme frost of minus two degrees as well as endless masses of snow it was not possible to bury the dead in a reasonably dignified manner. The soil was frozen too hard and too deep. Digging graves was impossible. The dead had to be simply left behind to save our lives.

Dramatic scenes were played out. The shoulders of the roads were lined left and right with the corpses of children and babies wrapped in blankets as well as dead old women and men who could no longer cope with the immeasurable exertions. It was unimaginable and ghastly what happened in these days, weeks and months at the beginning of 1945 in the east of the German Reich.

These images have burnt themselves deeply into my soul. We soldiers helped where we could, but we were impotent ourselves in many matters and had reached the limits of our own capacity to suffer and to perform.

In the meantime, the military decision had arrived in East Prussia, too. The Soviet attack started on 13 January between Nesterov (Ebenrode) and Dobrovolsk (Schloßberg) and led on 18 January to a breakthrough to the Instrutch (Inster) River that forced all German troops north of the breach to retreat behind the River Deime. On 22 January Insterburg fell, and on 25 January all East Prussian districts west of the line formed by the Deime, the Masurian Canal and the Great Masurian Lakes were already in Russian hands.

No less successful was the Soviet attack made from the River Narew bridgehead at Pultusk. By 19 January Ciechanow and Szkotowo (Soldau) had fallen and the East Prussian border had been crossed by Russian troops in the Neidenburg district. The same day the first Soviet units reached the districts of Szczytno (Ortelsburg) and Osterode and continued their advance toward Olsztyn (Allenstein) and Elblag (Elbing). Soon the towns of Olsztyn (21 January) and Mohrungen (23 January) fell and on 23 January Russian tanks temporarily entered Elblag, which was, however, only taken on 9 February after fierce combat. On 26 January the Russians had reached the Vistula Lagoon near Tolkmicko (Tolkemit) and thus interrupted East Prussia's land bridge and rail link to the Reich.

Only a small part of the East Prussian population had managed to cross the Vistula to the west before East Prussia's encirclement. Any further refugee movement to West Prussia had now become impossible, and as a last resort for the trails moving west in the central part of East Prussia only Sambia with the port of Baltijsk (Pillau) remained, and most of all the frozen Vistula Lagoon and the Vistula Spit, which offered a last land bridge to the west.

On 26 January the Deime position east of Königsberg had to be given up and Russian troops could then push into Sambia before encircling Königsberg on 31 January. Meanwhile, the 4th Army serving under General Hoßbach had left its position along the Great Masurian Lakes in forced marches in order to break through an encirclement of East Prussia in an offensive operation undertaken against the will of the Führer's headquarters and to regain alignment with the German troops standing west of the Vistula. After initial successes this attempt had come to an end on 26 January with Hoßbach's dismissal and the cessation of the operation initiated by him.

On 30 January the occupation of the East Prussian territory by concentric Russian attacks from the east, south, and west had already advanced a long way. The line along which the German troops were standing at that time ran from Tolkmicko at the Vistula Lagoon in a south-eastern direction to Orneta (Wormditt), then turned east and followed the avenue via Lidzbark Warminski (Heilsberg) to Bartenstein, from where it turned back in a north-western direction to Brandenburg near Königsberg close to the Vistula Lagoon and then continued inside the siege circle around Königsberg.

In this tubular pocket, which pressed against the Vistula Lagoon and encompassed at its centre the districts Braunsberg and Mamonowo (Heiligenbeil), hundreds of thousands of refugees were squeezed together. In endless trails they set forth from there on their dangerous route across the ice of the Vistula Lagoon. Besides the pocket south of the Lagoon, the city of Königsberg as well as western Sambia with Pionersky (Neukuhren), Svetlogorsk (Rauschen), Baltijsk (Pillau) and Fischhausen were still in German hands. Here countless refugees had also gathered.

These last German bastions in East Prussia were defended with extreme tenacity in the following month in order to gain time for the transport of the civilian population across the Lagoon and from the maritime port of Pillau (Baltijsk). It was 25 March before the last German troops crowded together on the Balga peninsula left the Lidzbark Warminski pocket across the Lagoon. On 9 April Königsberg fell and on 25 April Pillau, while on the Vistula Spit German troops held out until the armistice of 9 May.

Meanwhile, a similar split of the German defensive front and clusters of German troops and refugees in individual pockets had also occurred in the Baltic territories farther west around Gdansk and in Pomerania.

The same Russian advance that had seized with its right wing Szkotowo, Osterode and Elblag, aimed with its left wing along the northern bank of the Vistula toward the west. On 23 January Thorn was encircled, which held out until 30 January. Prior to that Bromberg (Bydgoszcz) had already fallen into Russian hands (27 January), and soon Soviet tanks had also reached Graudenz (Grudziadz) Fortress which was tenaciously defended until the beginning of March. Roughly at the same time as the Russians took Elblag, Marienburg (Malbork) was reached so that at the end of January the Nogat–Vistula line from Elblag to Grudziadz was in Russian hands. Near Grudziadz the front turned far to the east across the Vistula, where during the last days of January Schneidemühl (Pila) had been encircled (it capitulated on 14 February) and the first breaches of the Red Army had taken place into the South Pomeranian districts of Flatow (Złotów), Deutsch Krone (Walcz), Netzekreis (Czarnków-Trzcianka), Friedeberg (Strzelce Krajenskie-Drezdenko), Arnswalde (Choszczno), Pyritz (Stargard) and Greifenhagen (Stargard). The Soviets then tried to reach Szczecin and the mouth of the Oder, but these attempts failed for now because of determined German defence.

During the entire month of February the front in Pomerania and West Prussia came to a standstill about 50 kilometres north of the Warta–Noteć line with only minor changes. The mouth of the Vistula, Gdansk and the northern districts of West Prussia as well as Eastern Pomerania hence remained open as sanctuaries for all German troops and parts of the population who came from East Prussia across the Vistula Lagoon and Spit and from the southern part of West Prussia, or had been ousted from the Polish territories. Only at the beginning of March did the splitting of Pomerania begin.

On 1 March Russian spearheads reached the Baltic Sea coast near Köslin (Koszalin), thus barring the way to those fleeing west in the Gdansk region and the eastern districts of Pomerania and forcing them to turn back east, where there was still a possibility to escape via the ports of Gdansk and Gdynia. For the civilians and the German troops in the western half of East Pomerania the escape route and retreat across the Oder towards the west was more and more hemmed in during the first days of March, until here the land route to the west was cut off for good on 10 March, too. Only the town of Kolberg (Kolobrzeg), which only fell on 18 March after a fortnight's siege, represented a last sanctuary from where numerous refugees and troops could still be brought west with the aid of ships. Once also Gdynia and Gdansk – encircled from all sides – had had to be given up on 27 March, only the mouth of the Vistula near Schiewenhorst (Świbno) and the headland of Hela (Hel) remained free of the enemy. Just like the Vistula Lagoon in East Prussia, these areas that were protected by their natural position could be held until the capitulation and used as the last starting points for sea transport to Rugia, Kiel or Denmark.

In Silesia the Soviet advances on the bridgeheads at Brieg (Brzeg) and Steinau (Ścinawa) had widened sideways so much that at the end of January all Silesian territory east of the Oder was in Russian hands. Also Oppeln (Opole) had fallen on 26 January. Only around Glogau (Głogów) did a

German bridgehead still hold out in Lower Silesia east of the Oder. In Upper Silesia parts of the industrial region east of the Oder were still fiercely fought over, after its centre with the towns Beuthen (Bytom), Gleiwitz (Gliwice), Hindenburg (Zabrze) and Katowice had already been lost in the last days of January. On 10 February, after three weeks of combat, the last German troops standing in the Upper Silesian industrial region had to retreat behind the Oder, where they then led an equally tenacious battle for the defence of the Ostravan industrial region until the beginning of April.

On 8 February the Soviet divisions standing in Lower Silesia along the Oder started a new attack on the west. Advancing from the bridgehead at Ścinawa and simultaneously crossing the Oder north of Głogów, after hard battles and German counter-attacks along the Bóbr River they reached Görlitz (Zgorzelec) on the River Neisse. Between Guben (Gubin) in the north and Penzig (Pieńsk) in the south the German troops retreated behind the Neisse. Only around Zgorzelec was a German bridgehead held. In the course of that Soviet attack Liegnitz (Legnica) had fallen into Russian hands almost without a struggle and on 12 February Głogów had been encircled. Simultaneously with the thrust towards the Neisse, a pincer movement by the Red Army began on 8 February from the bridgeheads Ścinawa and Brzeg, which after fierce struggles led to the encirclement of Wroclaw on 16 February. Also Jauer (Jawor), Striegau (Strzegom) and Schweidnitz (Swidnica) were captured by the Russians in mid-February.

After an attempt by the Red Army to cross the Neisse into Saxony was averted for the last time on 3/4 March in the tank battle of Lauban (Luban), the situation in Silesia in mid-February only changed in a negligible way. Głogów managed to hold out until the end of March, and Wroclaw only capitulated on 6 May, two days before the general capitulation.

At the beginning of March the front ran from Ratibor to the height of Opole along the western bank of the Oder and from there via Strehlen (Strzelin), Strzegom, Luban until the Neisse near Zgorzelec. In the second half of March the part of Upper Silesia west of the Oder was also almost completely occupied, and in Silesia only a small strip along the Bohemian–Moravian mountain range border remained in German hands until the days immediately prior to the armistice.

Corresponding to Silesia's geographic location and the course of the fighting, the Silesian population fled into two main directions: either in a western direction along the main traffic routes to Saxony or in a southern direction to the mountains, which were relatively easy to reach from all the regions of Silesia, and from there farther across the mountains to Bohemia and Moravia.

In all the regions inhabited by Germans east of the Oder–Neisse line fighting had essentially ceased at the end of March with the exception of some ports, headlands, fortified towns and mountain ranges.

With our few surviving parts of our troop we were still with Army Group Centre, newly formed on 25 January and renamed Army Group A after the breakthrough of the Red Army at the Vistula. The command was given to Lieutenant Colonel Ferdinand Schörner, who was very controversial due to his harsh leadership. His merits consisted mainly in the fact that he had managed to lead his troops west after fierce rearguard battles and had established a new defensive front at the Oder. In order to save the industrial region around Ostrava, he defended it with his troops in a twenty-day battle and inflicted a resounding defeat upon the Soviets despite his own forces being far inferior. The Soviet advance was slowed and temporarily halted so that during this window of opportunity hundreds of thousands of refugees could escape in relative safety from Silesia to the west.

Schörner had already distinguished himself as a lieutenant during the First World War with the German Alpine Corps at the southern front in the victorious twelfth Isonzo battle, together with the then Senior Lieutenant Erwin Rommel, the future field marshal known as the desert fox. He had studied philosophy and modern languages in Munich, Grenoble and Lausanne before the First World War with the aim of becoming a university lecturer, and he had passed his interpreter exam in French and Italian. Yet the outbreak of the First World War ultimately led him to an officer career and to all the fronts.

During these last weeks of the Second World War he led all units of troops under his command with an iron hand and caused fear and terror. As a commander he was feared and hated within our troop. The last weeks at the Oder front live in my memory as a wild chaos of blood, ruin and desperation. The whole brutality of a leadership, having become absolutely ruthless in its self-affirmation, turned against its own troops during the total collapse.

The inspection routes of the infamous General Schörner were lined with hanged soldiers. Mostly these were stragglers who had been separated from their units in the confusion and could not produce marching orders. They then were considered deserters and Schörner, accompanied by a 'flying summary court martial', held a short trial for them. His 'watchdogs', the field police, thus called due to the chains with which they bore nickel badges on their chests, unceremoniously strung them up at the next available tree as a deterrent or shot them at the next wall.

Furthermore, his henchmen combed through all the field hospitals and regular hospitals, always looking for 'shirkers' and 'malingerers'. Not only slightly wounded, no, even those with severe injuries were dragged from their beds and sent directly to the front. An inhumane harshness!

Schörner was promoted to field marshal by Hitler on 5 April 1945 and made supreme commander of the army in the latter's last political will dated 30 April.

For the final battles the army group commanded the 4th Tank Army in the Dresden–Zgorzelec region, the 17th Army along the southern Silesian Oder line and the 1st Tank Army following in the south on the elevated positions along the line Neisse–Jägerndorf (Krnow)–Ratibor–Ostrava. The last headquarters of the army group were from 28 March to 9 May 1945 Bad Welchow (Velichovky) in the 'Reich Protectorate Bohemia and Moravia'. The capitulation of the last intact army group of the Third Reich took place in front of the 1st, 2nd and 4th Ukrainian Fronts attacking from the east. Encircled in a pocket north-east of Prague, the entire army group went into Soviet captivity.

After the 4th Army Corps under his command had bled out at the beginning of May between Oder and Elbe, Schörner absconded just in time in a Fieseler Storch aircraft, which he kept ready at all times, to Mittersill in Austria and thus evaded the downfall.

At the end of February, after long wanderings through the vast Silesian landscape covered in snow, I and some comrades ended up in the region between Zgorzelec and Luban.

A few months before the collapse, on one of the last days of February, I received in the late afternoon the order from an older staff sergeant called Ramsauer from the Bavarian Forest to establish a connection to the scattered comrades of a neighbouring unit so that these could reinforce our unit. Their location was described to me with vague assumptions, but was ultimately unknown.

Without map and compass, I trudged laboriously through the deep snow in the indicated direction. In the shortest of time it became dusk, and no soul was to be seen far and wide.

After about an hour I stumbled by chance upon a lonely squaddie, who was suddenly standing before me, startled. I thought he could be a deserter, perhaps even from the bunch I was supposed to look for.

Nevertheless, I asked him: 'I have an order to look for a scattered unit supposedly here in this area. Have you seen anybody or could you tell me the direction to search in?'

'Here is no German unit. I suggest you continue looking in north-north-western direction,' he replied.

I had few other options than to follow his advice, and so I set off in the indicated direction. In this process, however, within the next two hours I completely lost my orientation in the hazy, monotonous, white-grey winter landscape. Fields, forests and the rolling hills looked all the same here. Just don't run into the enemy's arms, I thought to myself, when I suddenly realised in the dark and almost absolute, oppressive silence that I had lost my way completely. No Russians, no Germans; here was nothing but a snow desert, darkness and solitude. I was angry with myself because I had followed the advice of the apparently ignorant squaddie, who had perhaps deliberately sent me in the wrong direction. And how could I only have lost my way in such a manner? I usually had an excellent sense of direction.

What could I do now? I tried to orientate myself with the aid of the lichen on the tree trunks and trudged in darkness through forests and across fields in the metre-deep snow for at least four hours. In the white landscape, details of the terrain could only be made out hazily.

Suddenly, when it was far beyond midnight, I had the sensation that I was exactly at the same spot where I had encountered the stupid squaddie four hours earlier. Depressed, freezing and hungry, I squatted down and quenched my thirst by eating handfuls of snow. A little later, despite the fierce cold, I fell into a deep sleep in the middle of a thicket and thus somewhat safe from discovery.

When I woke the next morning at dawn, I saw a gloomy and diffuse winter sky without sun. It was full of snow clouds. Scanning far and wide, I saw neither humans nor houses. Without a map and compass I had no idea where I was, and much less where the rest of my unit was located. I decided without further ado to continue my way towards the south-west in the hope of meeting somebody and most of all of finding something to eat, for my hunger was incredible.

Roughly two hours later, around 10am, I saw from afar a figure in German uniform wandering about, towards whom I marched immediately, as fast as the snow-covered ground permitted. The man was just as surprised as me to suddenly meet somebody in this solitude, and when I came closer I recognised the rank insignia of a German captain.

Without giving me the chance to make a proper report, he asked me: 'Have you seen my car? I am looking for my car.'

This question I had to answer in the negative, but thought immediately that this was a moment of opportunity. What a blessing! A car to take me along and not having to go on foot. I attached myself to this seemingly totally confused officer and offered him my assistance for his search. Subsequently we milled around this lonely area without any shred of a plan, and behind every corner, behind every hill the captain said: 'Here it stood, it must have been at this spot,' or 'No, it stood here, I am absolutely sure, my car stood there.'

Towards noon this funny game became too dumb for me, and I let him continue on his own as I no longer believed his story. Nothing was to be seen of his stupid car despite us searching far and wide. I had the impression that the officer was quite happy to get rid of me. Presumably he was a lost soldier who was perhaps considered a deserter, or perhaps he was traumatised by the turmoil of war, had lost his mind and was now wandering about totally confused and disoriented.

Now I was standing here on a spot in the middle of nowhere and was even more confused than this morning. Without further ado, I decided to continue my journey to the south-west. It was simply enough to drive me to despair. I did not see a human soul, and late in the afternoon my allotted time had run out.

An unauthorised absence from one's troop for more than twenty-four hours meant at that time that one was considered a deserter. This situation was now causing me extreme unease, and a rising fear paralysed me. If I was now picked up by any unit or the field police, I had to expect to be hanged or shot as a deserter.

In this situation, strangely enough I recalled a sentence from the lessons by Lieutenant Engelmann during our training at the Gneisenau barracks in Coblenz. As a confident superior of steady character, he had taught us to act quickly and independently in dangerous situations. In this context he used to quote a maxim from General Field Marshal Liman von Sanders. The latter was commander of the German troops in Turkey, then allied with the German Reich. He had said succinctly and pithily: 'Who has scruples in all places will never arrive at any deed in any way.'

Suddenly I no longer had no longer any qualms about what I planned to do and abided by these words. In view of the collapsed front, the sheer hopeless situation and the end of the war that was to be expected soon, but most of all, however, in view of the danger of possibly being executed by my own field police units, I spontaneously decided to somehow get through to the west on my own. It was an incredibly risky undertaking, but I had no other choice in this undeserved situation. As it was still daylight, I laid myself to rest in the nearest forest and during the following nights I marched for hours, keeping enough distance from settlements, villages and farms. From now on I was considered a deserter. I was aware of this, and this state strained my nerves.

On the third day, but even more so on the fourth and fifth, I was so weakened by the lack of food that I gathered all my courage and at nightfall approached two adjacent lonely Silesian farmsteads. Hidden behind bushes, I observed the houses, and when I was certain that I would encounter neither Russian nor German soldiers there, I dragged myself to one of those farmhouses on heavy feet, starved, lethargic and totally worn out. Suddenly it was all the same to me, when I knocked at the front door.

'Please, please, let me in. I am hungry, have eaten nothing for days and am freezing.'

13

Flight and Captivity

I knocked at the wooden front door of the first of the two farmhouses. 'Müller' read the sign. After considerable time an older woman opened the door.

'Who are you and what do you want?' she asked warily, but not in an unfriendly manner.

In my estimate she was around the same age as my mother. In the background of the entrance hall stood her husband and a young woman, probably a daughter of the two.

I introduced myself as Fritz Sauer, told them that I was a lost soldier on the retreat from the front and that for five days I had been wandering around Silesia in search of my troop. Since then I had eaten practically nothing and therefore was asking for something to eat.

These warm-hearted people were evidently as much shocked as moved by my rundown looks. Appalled, they held their hands before their eyes and called: 'For God's sake, gaffer, come in!'

'Gaffer' was meant in this case probably as the sort of address someone would use to an old man. I must have had such a black face and been so dirty that the mother spontaneously said to me: 'I will make you something to eat, but please first go upstairs into our bathroom. There you may wash, take a bath and shave yourself. We will put fresh clothes in front of the bathroom door.'

I gladly followed her advice and, having taken off my uniform, I bathed thoroughly for the first time in a long while in the pleasantly warm water and washed my blond hair, which had grown quite long by now. My last full bath had been two years ago. I had taken it shortly before I had been released from the field hospital in Lippstadt.

After shaving off my quite heavy growth of beard, I put on the fresh civilian clothes lying ready in front of the door and went exhausted, but ravenously hungry, downstairs into the kitchen of the large farmhouse. When the

Müller family saw me suddenly standing in their kitchen after almost an hour of bodily cleansing, I amazed everyone by my miraculous transformation.

'Having come just now from hell, a prince is suddenly standing before us,' said the courteous housewife.

During the meal I recounted in detail the entire course of my life and described the great danger of the approaching front.

'When the front comes threateningly close, we want to flee together with the French Schneider family and their children,' Mr Müller said quietly, as if the enemy could listen in. 'The Schneider family comes from Metz in Lorraine and was forcefully resettled here into our lonely region after the French campaign and the occupation of Alsace and Lorraine in 1940,' Mr Müller continued.

I was soon sitting with all the inhabitants of the two farmsteads in the cosily heated kitchen with its blacked out windows on this late evening. Together we conferred about different alternatives for escape, the best escape routes and the best time.

It was a grand caring gesture of these amiable people that they did not send me away into the icy winter cold, but let me to stay, although they placed themselves in mortal danger by doing this.

They made me a bed in the barn inside a false floor. Below me were the stables and above me hay and straw. During the day I had to remain in my hiding place, and Lenchen, the family's eldest daughter, brought me my meals into the barn. In the evening after dark I was allowed to leave my hideout. Then we all met in the kitchen. The Schneider family were also there every time, and we listened to BBC London on the radio, the prohibited enemy broadcasting station. Therefore we were quite well informed on the current situation.

On the evening of the third day of me being taken in by the Müllers, German soldiers cautiously approached the farmsteads. Immediately I went to my hideout and crawled into the false floor of the barn. I could listen to much of what was being spoken and observe what was happening around me through a gap in the wooden floor. They were a motley crew of around thirty soldiers, who were mostly very young but with a few older ones. Led by a captain, these poor devils were being sent back to the front again. They asked for a place to sleep, and one half lay below me in the stables, the other half on top of me in the haystack.

During this night I was in a cold sweat out of fear of being discovered. Don't make a sound, don't fall asleep and start snoring! I did not get a wink of sleep that night and prayed to God that nobody would discover me.

Only when the troop quit the field at dawn under a great commotion and set off toward the east, could I take a deep breath somewhat reassured.

Only later did we become aware that my presence was extremely dangerous for me and my amiable hosts. At that time my discovery would have meant certain death for everyone.

The same evening we were listening to the news from BBC London again in the blacked out kitchen and heard that Schörner's troops had brought the Red Army to a temporary halt in their advance after the most recent battle in the Luban area. Some days later we learned that the Russians would not invade the 'Protectorate Bohemia and Moravia' for now, i.e. Czechoslovakia. All of us decided unanimously to risk our escape the following night.

Our route was to lead us to the south-west, in the general direction of Zittau with the aim of reaching the mountains and the Sudetenland.

Both families packed the bare necessities into one covered wagon each, drawn by horses. Grandpa and Grandma Müller were wrapped in thick blankets and put onto the wagon. The people had to leave behind their house, outbuildings, land and possessions with a heavy heart. Among these were, of course, the animals. Since I could ride, I was gifted a horse that otherwise would have been left behind. We decided to stay together only for the first night. On the one hand I would make better progress as a single rider, and on the other hand if I stayed with them I would endanger my hosts if the field police stopped us.

In the evening we took our last hot meal together and set off around 9pm. For the Müller family it was farewell forever to their Silesian home, for the French family Schneider and me it was an attempt to return to our homes. For the whole night we travelled silently through the expanse of the Silesian landscape deep under snow with the exception of a few brief breaks. Only the creaking of the wooden horse wagons and the snorting of the animals could be heard. At dawn I said farewell to these amiable people and expressed my gratitude for the caring hospitality that had ultimately saved my life.

We all embraced for one last time. 'We wish you the best of luck on your long journey home, Fritz,' all of them called after me.

'I promise you that we will see each other again after the war, God willing,' I called back, deeply touched.

The trail of my trek led me further south to the Sudeten region. I continued my ride north of Zittau towards the south-west, carrying a backpack filled with some clothes and food. Before noon I reached a large brook of at least three to four metres across that was not entirely frozen. Later I learned that this was the little river Mandau (Mandava). I could see not see either a bridge or planks, so I decided to ride across. Usually, stretches of water of this width do not mean an insurmountable obstacle for horses, but my four-legged companion wanted absolutely none of this crossing. The animal shied every time I steered it towards the brook. The nag simply did not want to go to the other side. Probably it was frightened of the partly frozen edge of the water. Time and again I made another attempt, until the animal suddenly had enough. The horse shied once more, reared up and threw me off in order to gallop away at a leisurely pace. I believe that I ran after the horse for more than half an hour trying to catch it. When I finally caught the head collar, the animal made a circular movement with its head, pulled its head out of the loosened tack, neighed loudly and galloped away for good.

Now I was standing there without a horse, the head collar in my hands and still on this side of the brook. I had no choice but to take off my shoes, socks, trousers, including the long johns, and to wade through the ice-cold water to the western bank. After this involuntary refreshment I waited on the other bank until my trembling feet and legs had dried somewhat through my own body heat. Then I quickly put my new civilian clothes back on and was able to continue my long way towards the west without interruption, albeit on foot again and without the aid of this traitorous horse.

Toward the evening I spotted a small village and noticed a man of roughly my age just a few steps away. I approached the man, who was in civilian clothes, and asked him: 'What is your name, where have you come from?'

'I am Hermann and I am a lost soldier of the 4th Army Corps. After the death of almost all my comrades I have just battled my way to here. I know this area well. I am on my way home to Nixdorf (Mikulášovice), my home in the Sudetenland. It is approximately 30 kilometres from here. You can accompany me and stay the night with us. We only have to cross the old Reich border at the end. If you believe the latest news the Red Army will not cross the border into Czechoslovakia for now.'

Being absolutely unfamiliar with the area, I took up this well-meant offer without hesitation.

'I am in,' I called to Hermann with relief, and so during the following night we marched together across the border, unseen, and reached Nixdorf the following afternoon.

Hermann's parents had until recently owned a spinning factory whose operation had ceased weeks ago. The joy of seeing their son again alive was immeasurable. Here, too, I was received very cordially and fed. Nevertheless, I was advised to leave this place as quickly as possible, since not only was this family endangered by my presence but, far worse, Czech free corps and gangs harassed the German population living here, torturing, killing and deporting them. Everything German was hated and condemned. Even here in this little corner of land surrounded by the Reich border, life was no longer safe.

During the third night I risked further flight after close consultation with my hosts, who once again provided me with some food for the journey. The route that was closely described by Hermann's parents led, after a renewed crossing of the border, through the Elbe Sandstone Mountains and along the Kirnitzsch Valley to Bad Schandau on the Elbe.

After I had reached that river, I was relatively happy and content to have arrived back in civilisation. Downriver from Bad Schandau was Dresden, approximately 50 kilometres away. From there, I hoped, trains would travel west, and so this city was my next destination. I did not anticipate what was waiting there for me.

Having arrived at the edge of the Dresden suburb of White Hart (Weißer Hirsch), even from afar I could see such an apocalyptically destroyed city as I had not seen anywhere else before. The sight became unbearable on my approach and at close view. Whoever had lost their ability to cry, found it again through the sight of this horribly bombed city. The so-called Florence on the Elbe, once one of the most beautiful cities of Europe, a city of arts, had ceased to exist.

Downtown there was no sign of life whatsoever. What horror have the people in this city had to suffer! Still taking in this ghastly sight and lost in my own thoughts, I ran straight into the arms of a Russian patrol. There could be no thought of escape in the devastated streets of the city, and I was extremely angry with myself about my carelessness. Without asking me any questions, together with numerous other men and women I was integrated into a large group of prisoners. We were then led on foot for about eight kilometres to a railway area. Here there were two trains consisting of many rotten freight wagons. We were crammed into one of these wagons with loud Russian commands, shoves and kicks, and none of us knew what was intended for us. It looked very much as if we were to be deported to some kind of prison camp, perhaps even to Russia or Siberia.

The women and girls of my age were terribly frightened. They were captured Red Cross nurses and Blitzmädchen (lightning girls), i.e. telephonists and radio operators, who as the only women in the Wehrmacht worked in the telephone exchanges behind the front. We crouched on the bare wooden floor of the freight wagon. There was nothing to drink and no way to relieve ourselves, unless in a corner of the wagon.

I assessed my current precarious situation and considered it hopeless. Nonetheless, I was constantly on the lookout for a chance to escape, but a real opportunity did not exist at that moment.

Toward evening at nightfall, five bellowing sozzled Red Army soldiers with a rank smell of vodka opened the sliding doors, pointed their machine pistols to two young nurses and dragged the girls from our midst screaming in deadly terror into the open.

Through the open sliding door of our train wagon we all heard their terrible screams during their gang rape. Not far from us, just next to the tracks, the drunken brutes savaged the young blonde girls. The scene was grim. At the end some shots were fired, and the screams fell silent. The brutal soldiers had simply shot the poor raped women.

Now there was no holding me back. In the darkness that had fallen in the meantime, in the spur of a moment, I jumped through the open wagon door next to the tracks and ran across the railway in a sprint for my life. No shots were fired, and nobody followed me. Apparently the guard detail was not only satisfied but so drunk that they did not register my escape. I decided to give the city a wide berth and continued my journey west. Hereafter I avoided settlements and human contact for now. After a considerable time my way led me past the town of Frciburg toward Chemnitz.

After four days and five nights – during the day I rested and at night I marched – I took new heart and ventured onto public roads a little behind Chemnitz. These were overcrowded with people: civilians, refugees, former soldiers in civilian clothes, Russian soldiers and military convoys. As I was just twenty-one I looked adolescent and therefore hoped not to draw any attention.

I had not been marching alone for long on the crowded road, when two young girls with their bicycles stopped beside me for a short rest. One of them rode an old Miele bike, the other an even older Fatherland ladies' bike.

'We are both on our way to Gera. Do you feel like coming with us?' they asked.

They perhaps made this invitation out of sympathy, perhaps for their own protection; young girls were certainly vulnerable at that time. In any case, I took an instant liking to the two, and moreover we were heading in the same direction anyway.

'I would like to come with you and will ride your bikes in turn,' I called to them gladly. Thus the respective bicycle owner could spend this stretch of the journey on the carrier and rest, while I used the pedals.

We had a lot of fun and cycled cheerfully toward Gera. Admittedly we did not make fast progress on these old heavy boneshakers without gears. Yet we did not care much. 'Rather badly ridden than well walked' was our motto.

The Miele bike on which I took my turns had, however, a bent fork, which had the consequence that one could still cycle straight, but could not turn sharply right any more. This did not bother us much, since the road to Gera was straight. We sang hiking songs and enjoyed our freedom. There was no longer any fighting where we were travelling through, and the end of the war was probably near.

It was astonishing that we made it into Gera without meeting any checkpoints. Yet on a hill in the city our journey came to an abrupt end when we were suddenly stopped by a Russian four-man military patrol at machine gun point.

Immediately a pock-marked soldier with Asian facial features whipped the bike out of my hands.

'Give me bike,' he shouted. He probably came from one of the Turk republics of the Soviet Union. '*Dawei, dawei*,' he yelled at the two girls and chased them away. The girls ran as if the devil himself was after them. I could only gaze wistfully after them, while I was arrested by two Russians. Meanwhile, the pock-marked Asian proudly hopped onto one of the bikes taken from us, probably for the first time in his life. I just saw him riding fast down the steep road into Gera and realised that the Fatherland bike was lying in front of me on the cobbles. The man was hence riding on the Miele bike, which was incapable of turning right, and he was heading straight for the first sharp right turn at a relatively high speed. In vain he tried to steer right and plummeted with the bike over a low parapet wall and down a steep embankment while flipping head over heels several times. His comrades laughed gleefully, but he must have injured himself badly for I never saw him again.

In the meantime I was led at gunpoint to an open military vehicle, and I was taken a fair way outside the city to a military unit encamped there.

After a longer period of waiting, I was led into a fairly large tent, which I considered to be some kind of command centre for the unit. There I met a middle-aged Russian officer.

'I Major Valentinov am,' he introduced himself. Also present were two guards and another soldier taking minutes.

'How is name, rank and profession? From where you come? What division, where fought last years?' I was asked by this apparently calm and serene man in broken, but clearly understandable German.

Without inhibition, I told him roughly my course of life. While doing so, I recalled once more my apprenticeship as a hairdresser: after finishing school in Bassenheim I was discharged at Easter in 1938, while at the same time my brother Peter was drafted to the Reich Labour Service.

Beforehand Father had set the direction for my further course of life regarding the profession I was to learn. At that time practical professions were sought, since in the end they brought advantages for all the family. For boys these were, for instance, the classical crafts such as confectioner, baker, butcher, cobbler, tailor, cabinet maker, carpenter, roofer and also hairdresser. My classmates who had the good fortune to be able to train in a profession as an apprentice chose such a path, while those who were not so lucky had to scrape by after a fashion as unskilled labourers.

Originally I was supposed to learn shoemaking with the Ringel family, who were living in our neighbourhood, but apparently a rival beat me to it, and so without further ado it was decided that I should take up the vacant position as an apprentice with the hairdresser Anton Giering in the neighbouring village of Ochtendung. I was not asked whether I liked this; as a fourteen-year-old boy one was still considered a child. The decision was made promptly and over my head and any objections were not tolerated.

As a result, on my first day of work, early in the morning I went on my own to the train station, caught the train to Ochtendung and walked from the station there down to the hair salon in Polcher Straße in order to begin my three-year apprenticeship on time.

Although before the First World War and during the Weimar Republic an apprentice's due had had to be paid, professional training was free of charge in the Third Reich, and with some luck one even received a small wage. In my case a free apprenticeship was agreed.

Mr Giering was a strict but excellent mentor, although he liked to have one too many drinks on occasion. I was taught everything constituting the hairdressing craft in a concentrated form and in the shortest of times. From the beginning I had to do all the basic tasks that came up, and among these were the regular sweeping and cleaning of the shop.

Somehow I gained popularity very quickly and was allowed to cut the hair of many a citizen of Ochtendung by myself. Naturally I had to assist in the ladies' salon, too, and in this way I learned the art of hairdressing for both men and women. Among the latter were arranging water waves and putting in perms.

On the one hand hairdressing was a pleasant profession, as you had a lot of contact with every conceivable and inconceivable kind of people. In addition, you could on occasion let your creativity run free.

On the other hand the work was very exhausting. You were on your feet all day, and the six working days lasted more than ten hours in the first year of the apprenticeship. You were not treated with kid gloves as an apprentice, were faced with many demands and were exploited to a greater or lesser extent.

Objections, not being bothered, whining or calling in sick were inconceivable for us adolescents then. We would not have dared or would have been ashamed to shirk tasks and responsibility in this manner. On the contrary! What needed to be done was done as well as possible. That ultimately strengthened our self-confidence, our character and our positive attitude to life.

To this was added that you had to take on responsibility at a very early age, as time and again the the salon was full but the boss was out for some reason. Then I needed to 'step on the gas' mightily. I had hardly shaved five gentlemen or cut their hair, when six new customers were sitting in line. The whole day continued in that manner and ten hours occasionally turned into twelve, fourteen, or even more.

My advantage was my speed, and thanks to it and to my popularity with the customers I earned lavish tips as a rule. Here it was revealed that this neighbouring village was significantly wealthier than my home parish. Naturally not every customer gave a tip, but if one was given, the amount varied from one or two up to ten Reichspfennig.

After saving up for a long time I accumulated a decent amount and I bought a new pair of good sports shoes in Mayen. I had dreamed of those for a long time as they were being displayed in a large shoe shop that I passed every week on my way to professional college. I felt that these shoes were practically waiting for me. It was a lofty feeling to fulfil a wish of my own with money I earned myself.

I liked going to professional college as it was a contrast to the harsh apprenticeship and a welcome change of scenery. On the train journey from Bassenheim at the foot of the Karmelenberg (a wooded cinder cone formed by a volcano) past Ochtendung via Kerben, Polch, Hausen and finally to Mayen I could admire the beautiful landscape of the Vordereifel in bloom. Hundreds of people were at work in their fields with all kinds of tools, horses, oxen and draft cows.

Seeing them stirred memories of laborious work in the field during my early youth. I was glad to be able to train as a hairdresser, although this was hard and exhausting in a different way. I still helped at home with the farm, of course, when during the high season many tasks had to be done, and if my time permitted.

Travelling past, I glanced up to the large Lady chapel on top of the Karmelenberg. This originated in the year 1662 and was erected by Casimir Count von Walpott. The name of the mountain was derived from Mount Carmel in Palestine and gained common usage, after Heinrich von Walpot (spelling from the twelfth century) had returned safe and sound to Bassenheim from the Third Crusade. I had to smile to myself when I thought of the peculiar ritual performed up there almost every year on Good Friday after the service.

After the conclusion of the religious ceremony, for inexplicable reasons the boys from Bassenheim and from Ochtendung locked horns every year, sometimes more, sometimes less seriously, which became a tradition just like the church service itself. As soon as the older generation were on their way home, the youth of both villages pelted each other with lava rocks, which were scattered in their thousands here around the eastern volcano of the Eifel. Ochtendung was twice the size of our village, and the number of stone throwers corresponded with this. On every occasion we were driven for two kilometres along the beautiful old avenue of trees from the fifteenth century and farther beyond through our forest towards Bassenheim and the large railway viaduct, 18 metres high, the so-called Huh Breck (high bridge). Here on the bridge we could find enough basalt stones on the track bed to return fire, so that a farther advance of the attacks could be prevented despite our inferior numbers. Luckily, to my knowledge there were never any serious injuries.

Later I recognised some of the stone-throwing boys in our hair salon. Now I could let off steam on their heads with comb, scissors and razor blade, and it cost me some effort to hide my glee during the procedure. Yet cutting their hair was a bloodless and painless affair – almost painless at any rate!

We young people of the 1930s had as little interest in politics as the youth of all generations. We simply had other things on our minds. The NSDAP with Adolf Hitler had seized power within the state in 1933, when I was nine years old, and our Bassenheim had 1,644 inhabitants. A local group leader and a local farmer's leader were appointed in the village, and the National Socialist Women's League and Mothers' Collective were founded besides the German Young People (for ages 10–14), Hitler Youth and League of German Girls (both above the age of 14). These organizations were not seen by us children and adolescents as coercion, but rather as a welcome diversion, as far as we had time at all to take part in their activities. That is to say, due to duties at home it was not always possible to visit all the events.

As a rule we played sports during these gatherings, marched cross country or learned songs, which we sang around the camp fire. In larger, wealthier parishes or towns this might have been different and more extensive. In general it gave us pleasure to undertake something meaningful together with youths of the same age. Boredom or idleness were foreign words to us.

Even in our poor parish a tangible economic boom set in. No paradisiacal times prevailed, but the poverty of the Weimar Republic was gradually redressed. Although the industrial towns benefited more from the economic recovery, even we in the countryside indulged in one or two little luxuries, for example in form of a 'People's Wireless' (Nazi-era radio) with which we heard music in the form of the Request Concert shows, which consisted of classical music, light opera and contemporary hit songs, but also current news and the pithy propaganda slogans of the NSDAP with their incessant stories about National Socialist achievements. And those were many: monumental buildings, motorways, aircraft, express locomotives, ships, airships (Zeppelins), automobiles, the Silver Arrows of Auto Union and Mercedes-Benz on the one hand, broadcasting, telecommunication, medicine, chemistry, physics, sports and culture on the other hand. Everything was presented in such manner as if humankind's progress was solely emerging from Germany and the latter was heading for a golden future.

I could very clearly recall the times when every day early in the morning, dozens of unemployed young men were sitting in a long row on the large wall in our Mayener Straße and waiting to earn some pennies as day labourers. After the 'Black Friday' in the USA and the following world economic crisis the number of unemployed rose to six million within the German Reich. In 1933 the number of unemployed had gone down to zero within a few weeks and months – at least officially.

Less spectacular, but characteristic of this period, the exclusion of the Jewish population from the life of the nation was carried out. It began unobtrusively with the renaming of streets that bore the names of Jewish personages. This happened, for example, with our Von-Oppenheim-Straße named after Count Abraham von Oppenheim and his wife Charlotte, who in the late nineteenth century had distinguished themselves as benefactors of our parish. Without moving we suddenly lived in Bismarckstraße no. 1, until in summer 1945 the street regained its old name. This event was discussed in our family, too, and my parents were not happy about it, but it was simply taken note of.

Then in the pogrom night from 9 to 10 November 1938 (also called Kristallnacht) numerous synagogues were set on fire or destroyed across the whole country. Luckily nothing happened to the Jewish families Heiman in Mayener Straße no. 25 and Simon in Charlottenstraße no. 3. These people were absolutely respectable Bassenheim citizens like the rest of us.

Among us there were no prejudices and no racism or anti-Semitism. Yet in 1942, only four years later, when all men aged between seventeen and forty, sometimes older than that, had to fight on all fronts in Europe and the villages and towns were half empty, the henchmen of the Gestapo appeared and deported these poor people to the extermination camps.

In January 1939 a tragic accident befell my family that has been on my mind my entire life, but especially during the war at the Eastern Front in my often desolate and hopeless situation. What had happened?

Neat and diligent, as my father was, shortly before going to bed late in the evening he checked if everything was in order. During this round he locked the yard gate and checked upon the horses, cows and pigs in their stables in our barn. When turning on the light in the horse stable, the lightbulb gave out. When Father entered the stable in the dark without speaking to the horses to call attention to himself, the animals took such fright that one horse kicked out backwards and hit Father in the belly with the full force of its two hind legs. We heard the commotion and the screams of pain through the old single-glazed windows in the kitchen and immediately ran outside. Father was lying on the ground moaning and holding his belly with both of his hands.

We cushioned the cart with straw, placed our father upon it, covered him with a coat against the winter cold and pushed him to our hospital 300 metres away where the injured were admitted and patched up provisionally.

Three days later I was due to go to professional college and travelled to Mayen as usual with the first steam train in the morning. In the afternoon I was called from the class to the telephone in the director's office. A nurse in holy orders from our hospital answered: she said it was urgent and I should come to the hospital straightaway as my father was in a bad state. Immediately I packed my things, ran to the east station of Mayen and returned on the next train to Bassenheim. From our station I ran as fast as I could the two kilometres down to the village and further to our hospital. My whole family had gathered, and when I arrived there, it seemed to me as if Father had waited just for me – for his Fritzje, as he called me still as a fifteen-year-old. We were faced with a distressing picture.

Father had a yellow complexion and was on his deathbed, as everyone could see. The surgery carried out the day after his admission had been unsuccessful. The head doctor Dr Sauvigny tried his best, but spoke of serious internal injuries and a large rupture of the liver.

Three days after his accident, late at night, Father said his farewells to each of us, tortured by pain, and a little later closed his eyes forever. He was only fifty-eight years old. I felt like the saddest person on earth. The following funeral, however, felt even worse to me.

Hans took over our farm so that we could go on somehow. When time permitted that we could help with the work, Karl and I or even Peter on his leave mucked in without grumbling. Our mother, a widow at only fifty-six, fortunately had four strong sons who could all knuckle down.

In spring 1939, shortly after Father's death, my master, Anton Giering, was drafted to the Wehrmacht. However, since at that time in order to fulfil his apprenticeship agreement a master had to be present in every business for training, and since Mrs Giering was an excellent hairdresser but had no master craftsman's diploma, I had to change to a different master for the remaining two years of my apprenticeship according to the statutes of the hairdressers' guild.

Within a few days I received a position with master hairdresser Walter Stilling in Rheinstraße no. 30, just opposite Göben Square – today Görres Square in the historic town of Coblenz. It all went without a hitch. Everything was organized and nothing was left to chance.

For me this change was an exciting and welcome new challenge. The hair salon was in one of the best locations in town and was larger, more attractive and modern. Especially pleasant were the fixed working hours. I now visited the professional college in Coblenz once a week. Also, the urban customers were more diverse, most of all in spring and summer 1939 when many tourists came to Coblenz, and thanks to my intensive first year of apprenticeship I could step into the work at full capacity.

Of course, I still learned further techniques and hairstyles that I immediately began to apply, which earned me generous tips from the even more generous customer base. Here five or ten Pfennig were frequently given, which with a large turnover of customers was extremely lucrative. As a result I could buy my first suit from my own money after just a few months, and in Coblenz there were really terrific shops with fashionable clothes. I liked in particular that Mr Stilling paid me one Reichsmark per week from the second year of the apprenticeship onwards, i.e. four or five Mark a month. I found this fabulous, as I finally had the sense of being appreciated in my work.

Food in town was very expensive, though, and exorbitant for an apprentice. Therefore I took sandwiches along as ever. Yet since I was still a growing boy, Mother had an idea that we implemented two or three times a week. She insisted that I should have a hot meal at lunch for the long working day, and the procedure was the following: our business closed for two hours over lunch. Thus I ran to the station and travelled by train the 12 kilometres to Bassenheim. There Mother, Hans or Karl brought a pre-cooked meal to the station, which I was allowed to briefly heat up at the home of the amiable, large Schuster family and then eat in company at the family's table. Gertrud and Matthias Schuster were living with their six children Irmgard, Josef, Maria, Eduard, Christine and Susanne in one of the houses next to the station. Father Matthias worked for the Reichsbahn as an engine driver, drove his daily passenger train on the Coblenz–Mayen route and was familiar to me from my journeys to the professional college in Mayen, as he always leaned out of the steam locomotive when arriving at the station. It was always merry and harmonious in this large family, and I felt very comfortable and welcome there. Maria, who was the same age as our Karl, often helped out on our farm and felt at home with us. She earned some extra money in our small enterprise or received appropriate payment in kind for her work. I had to hurry my lunch, though, since the train in the opposite direction back to Coblenz left from Ochtendung when the train on which I had just arrived reached there. Exactly eighteen minutes remained to me for lunch, but that was enough. Then I travelled back to town and went from the station on foot back to the salon. What a hassle for a hot meal!

In the meantime more and more uniformed people were seen in town. Anybody who claimed to be somebody was wearing a uniform, at least it seemed that way.

Coblenz (Confluentia, derived from Latin confluere = to flow together; it describes the confluence of Moselle and Rhine) had been a garrison town since its foundation by the Romans in 9 AD, and this tradition became more emphasized in the current times. In addition to the barracks from the Imperial period, several new large barracks were erected within a short period. A zillion soldiers came here for their training and deployment, and they dominated the townscape. In the Rhine gardens and on the town squares, public concerts were frequently played by military bands, the theatre was always fully booked and numerous cultural events and dances took place.

Shipping on the Rhine boomed and the town was frequented by freighters and passenger boats. The town was decorated on many occasions, and in its bloom it seemed to me to be neatly arrayed, clean and liberal-minded. The displays of the shops were opulent and well-stocked. You could simply buy anything, even though much was unaffordable. Even exotic tropical fruits such as oranges, bananas and coconuts were widely offered. Nowhere did I get the impression of shortages.

Many tourists travelled on the big passenger ships along the Rhine to the Loreley, to castles and fortresses and also to our popular town. Until shortly before the outbreak of war one could meet many tourists from abroad along the Rhine, especially from Britain. Evidently the most German of all rivers was in great favour with the visitors. The romantic river landscape was rather popular. In particular I recall the many English ladies who displayed the then fashionable pale complexion, created by many layers of white powder.

The Rhine gardens were always full of people. All this I could observe while strolling through town during my break at lunchtime.

After the last French soldiers of the occupying forces had left Coblenz in 1929 as part of the Young Plan, the Rhineland became a demilitarised zone. On 7 March 1936, however, Hitler had the Wehrmacht marching in. This was followed by Austria and subsequently the areas predominantly settled by Germans in Bohemia and Moravia, sanctioned by the Munich Agreement, with which the French and British heads of government Daladier and Chamberlain hoped to assuage Hitler and thus to prevent another war. However, with the invasion of German troops of the rump Czech lands (Resttschechei) Hitler overstepped the mark. Although the western powers did not react with military resistance yet, they were nevertheless determined not to tolerate any further provocations by Hitler.

The disputes with Poland about the areas lost to it after the First World War and about the Free City Gdansk in particular were heating up in the course of 1939 and found their climax in the raid on the broadcasting station Gleiwitz (Gliwice), with which Hitler provoked a cause for war and began the Polish campaign in the conviction that Britain and France would only react politically, but not militarily. Yet the gambler at the head of the German Reich had been wrong.

On 1 September 1939 the German invasion of Poland triggered the greatest catastrophe of all times, the outbreak of the Second World War. It was a war so cruel and devastating as humankind had never experienced in its long history before and hopefully need not experience ever again. At the end almost 60 million people had met a violent death – an unimaginably, dreadfully high number.

With this renewed aggression the appeasement politics of the Western Allies, who had tolerated repeated military occupations and violations of international law by Hitler, came to an end. The German dictator had overplayed his hand. Two days after the attack by the Wehrmacht on Poland without a declaration of war, Britain and France declared war on Germany – something that Hitler had hoped to avoid as his geostrategic plans were directed toward Eastern Europe, where he wished to conquer further 'living space' for the German people.

Within only two weeks the Polish army was overrun by the then technically modern, well-equipped German Wehrmacht. One could follow the success stories all the time on the radio, in the newspapers and the weekly newsreels.

I myself and many people around me were not happy about this though. On 8 September, seven days after the beginning of the war, we in Bassenheim received the first notification of a death. It concerned the Braun family, whose nineteen-year-old son Georg Johann had been killed in Poland near Biskuzice.

The people in the village were upset and mourned together with the family, especially since a great number of husbands and sons from numerous other families had already been drafted into service with the Wehrmacht. That Georg was only the first in a long row of young men from our parish who would follow him into death, nobody could foresee when the so-called Blitzkrieg was concluded victoriously after just under three weeks.

The supreme command celebrated the triumph with all-out propaganda. That the campaign had also cost 10,000 fallen German soldiers and a multiple thereof in wounded people marked for life was not mentioned. These thousands of affected families were not in the mood to celebrate after our victory over Poland, nor were most of the other Germans. Unfortunately this limited and short campaign was only the beginning of a long period of suffering for those of Europe's nations that were drawn into this war.

Even greater were the losses of the Polish people, especially since, to the great misfortune of the Poles, the Red Army occupied East Poland immediately after the surrender of the last Polish troops as part of the Molotov–Ribbentrop Pact, so that the Polish state no longer existed. For the first time in this war the civilian population was affected to a considerable degree, too. The Polish capital Warsaw had been bombed to a devastating effect by the German Luftwaffe, in particular by the Ju 87 dive bombers.

Britain and France continued to sit idly by while their Polish ally perished. They were probably taken by surprise by the speed of the Blitzkrieg. They also gave a completely free rein to the second aggressor, the Soviet Union. And while many of the war crimes committed by Germans were punished with the utmost severity after the defeat of the German Reich, the crimes of the Communists, notably the cruel mass murder of Polish officers at Katyn, remained unpunished.

So now we were in the middle of a war, but as yet we did not feel its lash directly – for now. Nobody from our village wanted it, as the First World

War, during which fifty men from Bassenheim had fallen, was just twenty-one years ago.

After general mobilisation the cohorts concerned were drafted one after another: first to the labour service, then to the Wehrmacht and other institutions important for the war and armament effort. For this reason more and more men were drafted from our village. The younger cohorts were sent for military training to the barracks and training grounds. It was a duty that tolerated no exceptions. Any attempt to refuse to fight would in all likelihood have ended fatally. The absolute majority of us, and this is undisputed, would rather have remained at home and pursued their usual work.

Military service meant at that time commitment, honour and espousal of the Fatherland, as it had been carried out by all our fathers, grandfathers and previous generations, and as it was also common for the armies of other states. The pride, sense of honour and upbringing among young people at that time did not even allow the thought to arise of excluding and isolating oneself or being different from millions of other adolescents in Germany, France, Britain, in short Europe, and in many other nations of the world. If dangers or conflicts loomed due to tensions, regardless of the causes, whether deliberate or inadvertent, whether justified or unjust, the majority of my generation stood up for their nation.

The jingoism of the daily propaganda may not have left us unaffected. In my wider environment of family, friends, classmates and most of the population in our village, however, scepticism toward politics aiming to subjugate other nations and to kill their people prevailed.

I continued my apprenticeship in these tense, uncertain times, however, and studied diligently for professional college. At home Mother, Hans and Karl managed our farm as well as possible.

In spring 1940 a provisional airfield for the Luftwaffe was erected in the shortest of time at the foot of our Karmelenberg, on the right side of the Reich road from Bassenheim to Ochtendung on the so-called Willow Field. After its completion the first Messerschmitt Bf 109 fighters arrived. Famous flying aces such as Galland, Mölders and Wick took their quarters in our village at the Villa inn, today's Schloßklause (Castle Den). The entire village was overcrowded with billeted soldiers, especially with mountain infantry (Gebirgsjäger) from Bavaria and Austria. The looming conflict with our neighbour France cast its shadow ahead and seemed inevitable.

In spring 1941 I finished my three years of apprenticeship as a hairdresser with a very good grade in theory and practice. So my lovely time with the amiable Stilling family in the Rheinstraße of Coblenz came to its end. I had not only found an excellent teaching salon, but had been received most cordially there.

In my report to the Russian major I did not leave out, of course, that my father had died in 1939, my mother was living on her own at home and my other three brothers were deployed as soldiers somewhere in France to my latest knowledge. I had not received news of my family for more than half a year, and I could only hope that they were still alive. I reported the truth in every respect, and merely shifted my place of residence by about 120 kilometres farther to the west, into the immediate vicinity of the French border.

At the end of the interrogation this good-natured and decent officer said to me: 'You hairdresser boy, now prisoner, *woina pleny*. You cut my hair.'

'Yes, Major Sir, I am happy to do so. Yet I will need suitable tools,' I answered.

'You wait,' he said, stood up and called some Russian orders from the tent.

After a few minutes a Russian corporal appeared with a huge leather suitcase. When he opened the lid, I could hardly believe my eyes. The suitcase was full of razor blades, scissors, combs, shaving brushes and hair brushes of the highest quality. Among these were soaps, hair tonics and perfumes of all the then established manufacturers. During the advance of the Russian forces they had manifestly looted 'come hell or high water'. To all appearances the Red Army had pillaged all the hair salons, chemists and pharmacies along their route on their stampede through the German eastern territories.

In any case, I found the tools of my trade of the highest quality. I had not exercised my craft so far with such partly silvered or gilded scissors and knives. This was now the crucial acid test for me, and I took great pleasure in working on Major Valentinov's head. He received a fashionable cut of western style with short back and sides from me, and in addition a clean shave with disinfectant and a spray with original Eau de Cologne. I even found a mirror among the accessories, and while admiring himself from all sides the man gave me a satisfied smile. The following cascade of Russian sentences I did not understand, but interpreted them as praise, since he clapped me on the shoulder and gave me a piece of bread, a tin of lard and a sausage in a bread pouch. After I had been relieved of all my personal items carried in my backpack at the beginning of my arrest, including my wristwatch, I now at least possessed something to eat.

The major was wearing his new hairstyle with apparent pride, with which he clearly distinguished himself from the mass of his most amateurishly shorn comrades.

After that I was allocated a place in a tent among simple Russian soldiers. During the first night we ogled each other with suspicion. It was at first an uneasy feeling to share my sleeping quarters with enemy soldiers, but this sensation abated quickly. The soldiers conducted themselves as generous victors. They did not do anything to me, but simply ignored me. A few trivial words were exchanged with me, which I understood at least in part thanks to my rudimentary knowledge of Russian. Being under Major Valentinov's protection, I was shown respect, and I did not experience any maltreatment. During food distribution at lunch the next day, where I was handed a bland, thin barley broth, my fine barbering skills had already made the rounds. Every officer of the unit wanted to have his hair cut by me. Immediately after my frugal lunch my mission to beautify the officers and junior leaders of the Red Army began. A suitable chair was organized for me, and I could start the extensive schedule unimpeded.

I enjoyed my task, and suddenly I felt as if I was back in my first year as an apprentice. I had lost nothing of my speed. The Russians were standing in a queue, and I hurried along without letting the quality of my work suffer. I had all of a sudden the same feeling as in my time with master hairdresser Anton Giering in Ochtendung, where on one day I had cut the hair of almost sixty men without a break (the master was in session in the neighbouring pub at that time).

All the Russian soldiers were fully satisfied with my arts of beautification, and I earned a lot of praise and cigarettes. However, when in the evening, after at least forty haircuts, I sought my sleeping place in the communal tents, my bread pouch with the food was nowhere to be found, though. As I had eaten nothing since the barley broth at lunch, I went to bed hungry as so often during the last months.

After I had resumed cutting the hair of the queuing soldiers by mid-morning the next day, I had the opportunity to report the theft to a Russian officer, who prior to this had asked me in rather good German how I was treated by his soldiers. On the same day I received my bread pouch back including its contents. The thief was found out promptly and then punished by being whipped with a riding crop – at least this is what I was told later.

My captivity had now lasted two months. In the meantime I had established myself as a kind of regiment hairdresser and witnessed the end of the war with this Russian unit and its daily barley broth. During good weather and sunshine I moved my work station outside. Although the conditions of my captivity were relatively bearable, I was overcome every night by homesickness for Bassenheim. Time and again, at every suitable opportunity that presented itself, I asked for my release home when shaving Major Valentinov or cutting his hair at regular intervals. Yet the answer was always a curt '*njet*' (no) or '*nitchevo*' (unimportant).

On a beautiful sunny day in the middle of May 1945 an incident occurred that almost cost me my life, me who by being lucky a thousand times had survived the last few years. I was just busying myself to cut the hair of a Russian officer outside in the most gorgeous sunshine when not far from my spot a heavy detonation happened down at the little river. What had happened? A Russian jeep with two men had driven across the bridge toward us, when in the middle of this structure a mine, hidden by our pioneer troops, blew up together with the little jeep. Both men were dead on the spot. My customer jumped up, drew his pistol from the brown leather holster, loaded and cocked it and aimed at my forehead. I let myself fall on my knees and pleaded for my life. Alarmed by the noise and commotion, the entire camp gathered together, among them also Major Valentinov, whose shouting was able to prevent my liquidation at the very last moment. On the same afternoon he ordered me to his office. He spoke to me like a paternal friend in his usual calm, broken German:

'My unit going back to Russia. All *woina pleny* soon coming in extra camp. From camp then deportation to Russia. You done much good work for Russian soldiers.'

With this he pressed a document, a so-called passport for the Russian sector, into my hands with words I would never forget during my entire life: 'You still child, you go to Mama home, *dasvidaniya*, Fritz, farewell.'

Moved to tears, I gave an orderly salute for the last time, shook his hand in gratitude and took my farewell likewise with the words: '*Spasiba, gospodin, spasiba* (thank you, sir, thank you). *Dasvidaniya*, Major Valentinov.'

14

The Way Home

The next day I set off for home without delay early in the morning, overjoyed about my suddenly regained freedom. My relief about the fact that I was no longer a prisoner, a *woina pleny*, was indescribable. Nothing could rein in my urge to set off home any longer. All I owned was the bread pouch with a little to eat, what I wore on my body – and the precious Russian passport.

Some locals whom I asked for directions recommended the old Reich motorway as the shortest route west. This former expressway was busy with traffic, albeit in a rather leisurely fashion. Pedestrians and numerous horse carts besides some Russian military vehicles accompanied me on my way.

On the first morning I attached myself to a friendly comrade who, equally furnished with a passport, wanted to go west.

'I am Arthur Dzykonski and come from Hattingen near Bochum. Do you want to travel together? I am aiming for southern Westphalia. I have somewhat memorised the map,' he said, describing his plan to me.

'Well, I am in. We have roughly the same route. I want to reach the Cologne region and from there my home,' I replied to my new travel companion.

Full of optimism, we covered the journey to Gera, Jena, Weimar, Erfurt and Gotha in only two days of marching. That amounted to a little more than 100 kilometres, and late in the evening I had the sensation of hovering half a metre above the road. The longing for home was so strong, however, that we did not mind the exertion. From Eisenach we turned towards the north-west so that we reached the area of the British occupation zone at the point where the American zone bordered it. In this sector no checkpoint existed, and we could continue our journey unhindered, partly on foot, partly as hitch-hikers on open trucks or horse carts, or on one of the totally overcrowded trains, standing outside on its footstep. After days, with much luck, we reached the Ruhr region without having been checked once. The Russian passport would have been of little use to us here in the British sector, and there was still the possibility of being taken captive again.

After we traversed Dortmund, Witten and the area south of Bochum, which like the entire Ruhr region showed considerable destruction through many bombing raids, I said goodbye to my travel companion, Arthur.

A few days later, after less than two weeks since my release from Russian war captivity, I was standing all alone in Cologne–Deutz on the eastern bank of the Rhine and, as astonished as shocked, was looking at the protruding black Cologne cathedral and the completely destroyed historic town.

The chorus of the popular vernacular song 'Ich möch zo Foß no Kölle jon' (I want to go to Cologne on foot), which the Cologne composer and songwriter Willi Ostermann had written in August 1936, sprang to mind. The melody was created in reference to the earlier High German song 'Longing for the Rhine', which Ostermann had composed for the UFA film *The Dream of the Rhine* screened in 1933.

Reaching this city after all the years of war and the inexpressible exertions and hardships of the last months released indescribable emotions inside me. My long yearned for dream to return to the Rhine someday had been fulfilled. Choked up, I sang this song with its stirring melody to myself, quietly and full of humility, while tears were streaming down my face.

> When I think of my home
> and see the cathedral standing before me,
> I want to turn immediately home,
> I want to go to Cologne on foot.

Although I had not reached my actual home yet, which was still roughly 100 kilometres further south from here on the other bank of the Rhine, I had at least arrived at my beloved Rhineland. I could hardly believe that, apart from a few exceptions, I had managed the huge distances from the Russian zone to here on foot. The longer I stared at the cathedral, soot-blackened from the firestorm of the nights of bombing, the more mind–boggling it seemed to me that I had survived all the horrors of the past largely unscathed. At the sight of the sullen great river I realised for the first time how young I still was and that my youth had actually not really begun until now.

I ought to be able to manage the last segment until home quite easily, but there was one considerable obstacle, and that was my long yearned for 'Father Rhine' itself. In Cologne all the bridges across the river had been destroyed, and there was only one provisional pontoon bridge erected by the

Americans, which was to be replaced by a makeshift pile bridge currently under construction. The congestion on both sides of the river was enormous but I went to the end of the huge queue to learn that nobody was allowed across the Rhine without a permit. Nobody could tell me where I, a passing traveller, could obtain such a permit without running the risk of being detained again.

Crossing the great river here did not seem possible, yet suddenly the hand of God that had sheltered me most so far seemed to help me another time. A young priest from Cologne–Mülheim had listened to my appeal to be allowed to cross and gifted me his permit for the day with the words: 'I wish you luck, my boy. I can run my errands on the other side of the river on another day.'

Overjoyed, I crossed over the makeshift structure to the left bank of the Rhine into Cologne's historic town. From there a footpath ran unimpeded farther upstream towards Bonn. Early in the morning, after a simple night's lodging in the shed of an allotment in the south of Bonn, I set off on my last leg of the journey of slightly less than 50 kilometres. Full of longing for Bassenheim and magically drawn home, practically driven even, I marched through Bad Godesberg, Remagen, Sinzig and Bad Breisig to Andernach. I felt as if I was being buoyed up by God's hand and my route along the Rhine toward home was the most beautiful journey of my life. Countless thoughts accompanied me on this last leg. What would wait for me at home? What had become of Mother and my three brothers? Was my hope of seeing them all alive and well realistic?

In Andernach I learned that a military checkpoint had been established behind the railway bridge at the entrance to Weißenthurm. Returning German soldiers without identification papers were being arrested immediately. I took heed of this warning and turned directly towards the bank of the Rhine shortly behind the Nette riverlet, which originates in Hohenleimbach neat the Nürburgring and empties into the Rhine above Weißenthurm. In this way I circumvented this checkpoint, followed the towpath along the Rhine and at the southern end of Weißenthurm made another 90 degree swerve toward Kärlich.

By way of the so-called 'Sträßje' – as this poker-straight, almost three kilometre-long road between Weißenthurm and Kärlich was and still is called – I reached the entrance to Kärlich late in the afternoon. Having arrived here, I went immediately to the first house on the left. Here lived my aunt Helene Reif, née Sauer, a sister of my father. The joy of seeing me again alive and well was great. Eating, drinking and talking could not prevent me, however, from setting off again after a short while on my very last leg of now only just under five kilometres. For this purpose I got an old bike from my Aunt Helene, and thus I cycled through Mülheim, following the lovely vale, past countless fruit trees and the Bassenheim brook towards my home village.

It was June 1945, and the cherry trees right and left of the way bore fruit in abundance. The gorgeous summer evening was filled with balmy air, peace and quiet. I felt like I was in paradise. That I came from hell was probably not detectable from my appearance. I cycled past the Waldmühle [forest mill], then the Burgmühle [castle mill], followed the long enclosure wall of the castle park, and then I could see the houses of our village.

When the first inhabitants of our village greeted me, the news of my return spread like wildfire through the place: 'Fritzje is back, Fritzje is here again.' People waved and called something joyful to me. I registered all this only subconsciously, however, and as if in a trance, I headed straight for our street and our house.

The gate to the yard and the door to our house were wide open. Nobody was at home, neither my mother nor my brothers. I walked through all the rooms and noticed that there was actually nothing left worth stealing. All the wardrobes were empty. None of us boys' clothes were left, just a few old dresses still hanging in Mother's wardrobe.

The emptiness of the wardrobes, I later learned, was the result of the prisoners of war who had been forced into labour taking all our clothes when they had been released to go home after the Americans invaded.

When I went downstairs, Mother was just returning from visiting my uncle Peter Paul – from the family who had to mourn so many fallen, as I learned a little later.

Our reunion could not be described in words. We fell into each other's arms in tears. It was unbelievable and could not yet be grasped at all. I was back home again and had survived the war with all its hardships and horrors. At that moment I was left with nothing and standing before a new beginning.

All at once I made my round through the stables in the barn outside, but what I found seemed strange to me. Our horses Fuchs (fox) and Elsa were no longer there. The pigs were not there, either. Apart from a few ageing chickens, nothing was left from our livestock. Instead, all the stable boxes were taken up by cows. After a short discussion with Mother I found out that these cows belonged to our local group leader Servatius. The latter had been arrested by the occupiers and thrown into prison, but prior to that he had stabled his animals on other farms – in part with us.

Full of anger, I grabbed the next available wooden club, opened all the stable boxes and under loud shouting drove all the cows across our yard onto the road. From there they now were ambling without any control through the entire village, but I did not care at all. Although Mother was mightily upset about it, I took great pleasure in it, as I had no inclination to look after the local group leader's cattle, the man who had inflicted so much sorrow upon us.

Late in the evening we told each other everything we had experienced in the last two years. Our conversation lasted until late in the night, and I felt no tiredness, although I had set off early in the morning from Bonn for my last leg of the journey.

In my momentary happiness it seemed to me as if I could forget the hardships, the suffering, the misery and the horror of this inhumane and terrible war. This was a fallacy, however, for the events and images caught up with me again months and years later – sometimes to a greater, sometimes to a lesser degree. It took many decades until the horrible events slowly faded with age. I could never really forget the horror and grief about my many dead friends and my lost youth.

I was the first of us four brothers to return home. Yet how had the others fared, and the many men from Bassenheim who likewise had gone to war?

For my eldest brother Hans, military service ran a rather unspectacular course. He served with an anti-aircraft detachment and after abandoning his weapon due to a lack of ammunition he became a French prisoner of war. In spite of some extremely dangerous missions while looking for mines he returned home unharmed in 1946.

Peter, my second oldest brother, was captured in Le Havre by the British, after his heavy coastal battery at the Atlantic Wall had run out of ammunition during the invasion. He was taken to a prisoner of war camp in England and was detained there under very humane conditions. After a certain time he was assigned to a large farm for labour due to his agricultural knowledge. Peter had quite a good stay with this English family. He was treated in a friendly manner, had adequate accommodation and enough food.

Yet his homesickness grew day by day, month by month, year by year. Decades later we discovered entries in his diary from this period. Here are two original examples from Peter's memoirs, representative of lines and poems written down by German soldiers in captivity out of despair and longing:

> Good night, Mother. Today a letter came which you wrote to me. Only a few short lines by Mother's hand that you love me travelled for thousands of miles. Suddenly you were so close to me and I was sitting at your feet, suddenly home was there with a thousand kind regards.
>
> Now it is late, you are tired, great were the labour and sorrows, your son is here, sings a song for you, sleep now until the morning.
>
> Good night, Mother, good night, you have thought of me in every hour, have worried, have agonised over your son and in the evening have sung a lullaby to me.
>
> Good night, Mother, good night. You have had worries and concerns.
>
> You love me Mother, you have watched over me, good night Mother, good night.

> At home a girl is waiting for me, she is my desire and happiness.
>
> She promised me to wait for me, she is my desire and happiness.
>
> And so I think of home, of mother and child, for I like her so very much.
>
> At home there is a girl crying for me, she is my desire and happiness.
>
> Now I am kept prisoner in English lands, the moon has just awoken.
>
> The stars in the sky, they are shining down, they illuminate many a lonely grave.
>
> And so it pulls me away toward home so much, my longing remains forever with you.

After four years of imprisonment and labour in England his dream of returning came finally true. After his release in 1948 Peter returned home to us.

With his great love Helene, whom he mentioned in many poems and verses full of longing, he lived happily in Bassenheim until the end of his life. They had two children, Norbert and Christel.

In contrast to our two older brothers, my youngest brother had to live through a veritable odyssey. During the invasion of Normandy on 6 June 1944, Karl was deployed with the 12th SS Tank Division 'Hitler Youth' at the hotspots between Caen and Cherbourg. Here his Panzer IV was set on fire after a few days and several skirmishes. The entire team escaped through the hatches and got to safety despite enemy fire. Karl suffered substantial burns on his legs in the process.

After returning to their unit, the tank crew received a brand new tank of the Jagdpanther type, equipped with a powerful 88mm cannon, and was sent anew into battle. With this modern combat vehicle – one of the best during this war – they destroyed nine American Sherman tanks in no time, which were far inferior in combat power to the latest German types, the heavy Tiger and the moderately heavy Panther. Many hounds soon catch the hare, however, and at the time of the invasion there were thousands of hounds and only a few hares.

Shortly after these successes, the head of Karl's tank commander, who led the battle from the open hatch to get a better view, was torn off by a mortar. This man had been Karl's human and soldierly role model and in a certain way replaced our father, who had died far too early. This horrific event was the only situation during this war that made Karl cry bitterly.

Further missions with a new commander came to an end after only a few days due to a lack of ammunition and most of all fuel. The tank was set on fire by its own crew so that it would not fall into the enemy's hands.

Up to the capture of Paris in August 1944, 70,000 Allied soldiers fell, but during the first weeks after the invasion 200,000 German soldiers died. They were used as virtual cannon fodder in a hopeless battle against immensely superior forces. Karl was lucky and survived this inferno. Together with the remains of the 12th SS Tank Division he was pulled back from the front immediately after these skirmishes.

After brief replenishment the costly participation in the Ardennes Offensive followed, and after that his transfer to the south-eastern front in Hungary.

Once more furnished with the state-of-the-art Tiger and Panther tanks, this unit fought there with numerous other army units in the Battle of Lake Balaton. In the final phase of the fighting all the remaining tanks were set on fire or blown up due to a lack of fuel.

From Hungary Karl set off to flee home on foot ahead of the Red Army. In the company of his comrade Bernhard Martini from our neighbouring village Ochtendung, he wandered for weeks through Hungary and Austria via Wiener Neustadt and then Bavaria until he reached the area around Frankfurt at the Main. Here the two were taken captive by Americans and a few days after their arrest were interviewed in perfect German by an American officer of Jewish descent.

Afterwards they were stuck into a large camp on the Main meadows together with a zillion other German prisoners of war. Similar to the Rhine meadow camps in Sinzig, Remagen, Andernach und Mainz-Bretzenheim, many men died here for lack of food and water.

Karl was a heavily built man of rude health and gifted with Herculean strength, but inside this camp his weight dropped from 130 kilograms to half of that in the shortest of periods. As an involuntary SS member, after many weeks of imprisonment in the camp, he was brought to the prison in Dietz at the Lahn. Here former party bigwigs such as local group leaders, local farmers' leaders, SS members and other NSDAP members of various former organizations were predominantly incarcerated. After he had lost another five kilos there, he was transferred to Linz on the Rhine. There he recovered somewhat and in autumn 1945 I was able to personally go and collect my brother and bring him back home.

During a later dance event Karl used the opportunity to confront our former local group leader Servatius with the events that had led to his enlistment. After Servatius had pushed Karl away and torn his shirt in the process, a serious brawl took place outside in front of the pub before a large crowd, after which Servatius could only limp through our village supported by a stick.

Yet was not he ultimately a victim of these times, too? Perhaps for him, and the likes of him, it was much harder to continue living with his conscience after the catastrophe and the uncovering of the horrific crimes of the Nazi regime than for others with a relatively clear conscience who could claim to have known nothing and to have suspected little.

In the end we in our family were enormously lucky with the return of all four brothers, in contrast to many other families in the village.

Especially hard hit was the family of my uncle Peter Paul. Four of his sons were deployed at the Eastern Front. Heinrich fell in December 1942 at Stalingrad and Georg in November 1943 at Libartowo. After these losses their brother Hermann was withdrawn from the Eastern Front in summer 1944 and classed as an essential home worker. He was allowed to return to Bassenheim to work his family farm.

In autumn 1944 Hermann was ploughing a field with his horse on the Saffig Hill above Bassenheim. During this chore, bombs dropped from an American aircraft. Whether this was an emergency release or whether an attack was made on a lone labouring farmer could not be determined afterwards. In any case, the bombs hit the ground immediately in front of the horse, which was killed. The horse and steel plough acted as a protective wall so that Hermann remained unscathed apart from a few bomb splinters that tore up one of his calves in several places.

The ten-year-old Wilfried Frei was the first on the scene and together with his father brought the injured Hermann to our village hospital, erstwhile founded by Abraham von Oppenheim, which was only 800 metres away. At that moment of all times, anything more than minimal treatment by the religious nurses present, i.e. putting on a bandage, was not possible there. The head doctor Dr Sauvigny had been detailed to the Eastern Front as a division surgeon so that no doctor was present that day. Hermann was taken to the Brüderkrankenhaus Saffig (a hospital run by monks) the next day. A young and inexperienced doctor removed the bomb fragments from the torn calf. Disinfectants were barely available as the fronts devoured all such material and had priority.

The fatal result of this became quickly evident. After two days the entire leg far up to the thigh had changed to a black colour due to gangrene. In order to save Hermann's life the entire leg had to be amputated at once. Hermann survived the serious operation and did not lose his courage to face life. He later became director of the Raiffeisen Bank in Bassenheim and until his retirement limped back and forth the 200 metres between his house and his workplace four times a day. He bravely bore his severe disability during all those decades and mastered his life well. Hermann died on 12 December 2016 at the ripe old age of almost ninety-five.

Later in 1944 the family received the next bad tidings: their third son, Anton Sauer, had fallen on 15 November.

Furthermore, we lost our cousins Heinrich Caspar Quirbach and Albert Quirbach. Albert was a son of Uncle Gottfried. His two brothers, Erich and Heinz, survived the war, but only came back from Russian captivity after many years as late returnees and were marked for life. Apart from my relatives I had also lost my close friends Arnold Lohner, Edgar Weiber, Robert Kleinz and Herbert Niederländer.

Many small children in our village have never met their fathers. In a family with five children, often just the only daughter survived. The mother could not bear this loss and became depressed.

In our small community alone the senseless war claimed 114 lives. The largest part of these men fell in Russia. The others perished in Poland, France, Italy, on the seven seas, somewhere in captivity or in one of the many field hospitals. Many remained missing.

Many soldiers from our village had survived but were marked by serious injuries, under whose consequences they partly suffered until the end of their days. Many comrades had lost a foot, a leg or an arm, others received a lung or head shot or lost their eyesight. My handball mate Walter Ringel recovered almost completely after being shot in the head, so that he later played field handball with me in the Rhineland regional league and ran his bakery until retirement.

Alois Knipper, likewise a baker, was recovered seriously wounded by Russian soldiers. He survived his lung wound thanks to an operation that the Russian doctor performed without anaesthesia and with him being fully conscious. After his recovery he went into captivity and after his release likewise ran his business until old age. With much luck, Klaus Lohner survived the inferno of Stalingrad. After being wounded, he was one of the few who could still be airlifted out by a Ju 52. The loss of one eye affected him seriously for his entire life, too. Yet none of them and or any of the other returnees ever gave up on themselves. Most of them continued to work in their learned profession after their return despite physical disabilities, or they retrained for a suitable occupation.

There are a number of other fates that became known to me: Josef Reif, whom I met by chance for the last time in summer 1943 in Coblenz, remained with his unit inside the Courland pocket until the demise of the 132nd Infantry Division. He saved the life of our comrade Paul Wagner from Nörtershausen in the Second Courland Battle in November 1944 in the region of the Latvian–Lithuanian border south-east of Frauenburg (Frombork), when, endangering his own life, he rescued him seriously wounded from the frontmost line with the aid of a borrowed tank and transported him to the field dressing station. Only a few days later, on 25 November, under fire from Russian kaboom cannons, shrapnel almost tore off his entire left arm in the area of the elbow joint.

After rapid rescue and good initial medical treatment, he had the great fortune to be evacuated from the Libau port with one of the last navy ships and thus escaped the Courland pocket. The ship landed with 2,000 wounded soldiers on board at Gotenhafen (Gdynia) near Gdansk. After being taken in trucks from Gotenhafen to Gdansk, the wounded were allocated to two ambulance trains waiting there at the ready. The first went to Austria, the second to Saxony. Josef went to a field hospital in Dresden and underwent three operations performed by an excellent surgeon. His arm could be saved and later showed only slight impediments in mobility. Only thanks to this doctor, who forwent simple amputation and risked these then complicated procedures, could Josef carry out his profession as a farmer until his old age. On 9 September 2014 he celebrated his ninety-first birthday and died in May 2015.

My caring, paternal regiment commander of our 437th Regiment, Colonel Maximilian Kindsmüller, fell on 17 August 1943 east of Slavyanka near Leningrad at the age of forty-eight.

Paul Seidenfuß returned home with the usual physical and emotional wounds from war and captivity and practised his learned profession as butcher in Coblenz until retirement.

Ulrich Schmidt returned home after many years as a prisoner of war in Russia and after a long time full of hardships saw his wife and his son Uli again, the latter now an adult having being born in 1939.

Paul Severin was allowed to begin his studies in law during the war due to his arm amputation. After graduating he worked as judge at the district court Andernach until his retirement.

Jakob Schmitz survived his lung wound, but later suffered from chronic breathing difficulties. As he did not have to return to the front, he took part in the restoration of his heavily damaged home city of Cologne.

Georg Bauder was captured with his reconnaissance party at the Eastern Front and was sent to a Russian prisoner camp. After he had survived several years in various camps, he returned maltreated and deeply scarred for life in 1953 as a late returnee to his home city of Mannheim, then still largely destroyed. Due to the chemical factory BASF being located opposite, this city as well as Ludwigshafen were very frequents target of intense bombing raids. Georg's wife Lydia had waited almost ten years for her husband and suffered a nervous collapse at their reunion due to a combination of pain and joy. God gave the couple two girls and a son, and the family lived happily in the city risen from the ruins.

Georg, whom I always remembered as a wonderful, helpful and amiable person, never fully recovered from camp imprisonment and its hardships. After a long struggle he died of cancer and was buried in 1979 in his beloved home city. Lydia mastered her life without him for another thirty years and died in 2009 aged eighty-nine.

Our musical bureaucrat Klaus Baulig from the neighbouring village Mülheim, who knew how to play the violin very well, was one of the first of us to fall after his transfer to another unit in summer 1942.

Sergeant Engelbert Haymann, who with his comradely behaviour was always a role model to us, was transferred to an anti-tank battalion of the 'Greater Germany' Division and fell on 21 July 1943 during the summer offensive in the area of Army Group Centre near Belgorod. He was buried in a soldiers' cemetery near Kharkov.

Markus Heinrich received a shot in the backside and was flown out in a Ju 52. Yet fate led him to the Eastern Front a second time. There he witnessed the collapse in the fierce final battle of Berlin. With incredible luck, he survived this last inferno, initially battling his way north to Schleswig-Holstein and then to Bavaria.

Likewise, Toni Grad survived the war and after his captivity saw his beautiful Bavarian home again, too.

Alfred Frensch from my home village, whom I had met by chance at the Thorn station during the war, belonged to the few who returned from the war unscathed. He later lived with his wife Anna and their four children only 50 metres from us, and he died in 2012 at the age of 87.

Matthias Schuster, the friendly old engine driver from Bassenheim station at whose home and in whose family circle I had frequently taken my lunch, was in a train that was attacked by American fighter-bombers during a journey from Coblenz to Mayen on the section between Polch and Mayen in 1944. He and numerous other civilians escaped their locomotive and passenger wagons, but died in the hailstorm of bullets and bombs from the repeatedly attacking aircraft. Matthias left behind his wife and six children. His youngest daughter, Susanne, married an American officer after the war, who in civilian life was a dentist, and she went with him to the USA. She is still living there today at a ripe old age.

Arthur Dzykonski from Hattingen, my travel companion during the last days of flight, found my address by chance in a telephone directory after forty-six years. Immediately after there were several mutual visits from 1991 onwards together with his wife Gertrud and my wife Hermine, sometimes in Hattingen and sometimes with us in Bassenheim.

My lifesavers in Silesia, the Müller family and the French Schneider family, managed to escape. The Müllers later put down roots in Borken in North Rhine-Westphalia. Their daughter, Lenchen, became a Steverding by marriage and bore many children. The Schneider family returned to their home and lived in Metz. All three families and children visited each other regularly during the 1950s and '60s. Sometimes the meetings took place here with us at the Moselle in the Rhineland, or the journey was made to neighbouring France and Metz or to Borken. Time and again we exchanged memories. Indeed, only years later did we truly realise how close we had come to death.

My Italian fighter pilot friend Mario from Turin, whom I had met at the camp in Thorn and had sometimes helped out with food, I unfortunately never saw again. I would have liked to follow his invitation to visit him in Northern Italy. Yet the scrap of paper with his address got lost during my captivity, and in the post-war years I lacked both the time and money for extensive research, not to mention the travel costs. This was a great pity, for I have never forgotten Mario.

After the war there were in almost all the communities, villages and towns of Germany, Austria and South Tyrol memorials for the fallen and missing in form of plaques and monuments on cemeteries and central squares, although this was entirely neglected in Bassenheim for reasons unknown to me. Only in the 1990s, on the initiative of the local history society, was a small, unimposing plaque with the names of the fallen or missing soldiers from our parish put up on the left side of the entrance area to our church, and even this list was not complete.

In view of the German–French reconciliation long since accomplished in the private sphere, I delighted all the more in an event that occurred in my home village Bassenheim of all places.In 1948 the later Federal Chancellor Konrad Adenauer, together with his friend, the French Foreign Minister Robert Schuman, landed on the military airfield at Mendig. In darkened limousines they drove to a secret conference at Bassenheim Castle. Here the

French general Hettier de Boislambert was also residing as governor of the Rhineland-Hesse-Nassau prefecture within the French occupation zone.

During this discreet meeting the first German–French treaties of friendship were conceived, which happily were put into action between the two countries, or rather into many actions.

In 2012, in recognition of this wonderful deed by Schuman and Adenauer to unify our nations, a worthy monument was erected on our Walpot Square.

Today, Bassenheim maintains twinning arrangements with Pougues-les-Eaux in Burgundy and for the last twenty-five years with Pasym in Poland, the former Passenheim, which was founded centuries ago by Heinrich Walpot, a citizen from Bassenheim.

15

Rebuilding

Life awoke quickly again in the defeated Germany after it was liberated from the Nazi dictatorship. After a few years of hardship the economy, and with it the rebuilding of the destroyed country, gained momentum after the monetary reform of 1949 – at least in the Western occupation zones. The regained peace and the first democratic freedoms granted by the Allies gave the people hope and courage for a grand new beginning.

Everybody tried to build up a new existence according to their abilities. The destroyed cities needed huge capacities of labour and copious amounts of building material during their restoration.

Thus the pumice and sandstone industry located here in the Neuwied Basin experienced an enormous boom. In the beginning, still with back-breaking manual labour, a gazillion building stones were produced from the metres-thick pumice layer, which was situated immediately beneath the topsoil in this region, and which had formed in the course of several volcano eruptions 10,000 years ago.

My brothers Karl and Peter, as well as Josef Juchem, founded one of thirteen pumice factories to emerge in Bassenheim alone. In Weißenthurm even almost 100 of these factories were built in the shortest of time. If all the production sites of the surrounding villages, for example Ochtendung, Plaidt, Saffig, Miesenheim, Andernach, Mülheim, Kärlich, Kettig, Urmitz, Kaltenengers and on the other side of the Rhine Neuwied, Heimbach-Weis, Glattbach, Torney, Engers and many more were added up, there were probably around 400 stone-producing enterprises.

The advantages of these building stones made from pumice, sand, cement and water were their relative light weight, their insulating properties, their larger format compared to bricks, their affordable price and their almost unlimited availability. To this was added their easy transport due to the favourable traffic location on the Rhine and the railway lines on both sides of the river and near the Federal Roads. It can be stated here without exaggeration that a large part of the relatively prompt rebuilding of the Federal Republic was achieved with stones from our Neuwied Basin.

When at the beginning of the 1960s the building boom gradually abated, many of these small enterprises had to close. Following this, Karl worked as crane operator in shifts with the Thyssen Krupp company at the Sayn steelworks near Engers until his retirement. Whether in pumice production or at the steelworks, Karl, like numerous others who had returned from the war, contributed for decades to the rebuilding and progress of our country.

Despite hard work since early childhood, involuntary participation in the war, captivity and following heavy manual labour, Karl reached the blessed age of eighty-nine. He died on 8 July 2014.

In autumn 1945 I began to practise my hairdressing craft in the laundry room of my parental home. A little later I had enough money to rent a hairdresser's chair in Maria Beitzel's hair salon, by which I improved my surroundings considerably. After a further boom, and having passed my examination as a master craftsman as the youngest participant in the Rhineland, my money sufficed to rent two rooms in the Zur Krone pub, where today the savings bank of Bassenheim is located. Here I now ran a ladies' and gentlemen's salon together with my wife, Hermine, who for this purpose alone had learned the profession at the professional college in Duisburg and the international master schools in Duisburg and Rüdesheim. In 1955 we fulfilled our dream and opened a new and modern salon in Mayener Straße 39. I was still running this business at the age of sicty-six until the end of 1989.

In spite of my disability arising from the leg injury, the long hours of standing in this profession did not bother me in my younger years. Like many thousands of my comrades returned from this accursed war and marked on body and soul, I began my contribution to the renaissance of our country without complaint.

Afterword

Peace and freedom are not to be had for nothing! That was never the case in the history of humankind and that will unfortunately never be the case, either. Evidently this can be followed painfully and for real today in the countless old and frighteningly many new centres of conflict all over the world.

Across the millennia until our current times it has been proven and reasoned by historiography based on countless examples that through thirst for power, fanaticism, racism, religious mania, fundamentalism, nationalism, Communism, envy, jealousy, and also bondage, oppression and poverty, the breeding ground and the foundation stones are laid that lead to tension, escalation, destabilisation and war in all the facets of their potential excesses with their fatal consequences for humankind.

It lies especially close to Fritz's and the author's heart with this publication that such a tragedy such as that of the Second World War does not repeat itself; that we finally learn from the mistakes in our history so that wars are no longer being conducted.

After immeasurable suffering during six years of war, which the majority of the German people did not wish to conduct at all, but which was staged by a dictator and leader together with his closest vassals, Germany's liberation by the Allies was a blessing for the people in our country and in all of Europe. In particular, the Americans claimed for themselves the largest part in our liberation. Their reasons for this are not entirely unjustified: they brought democracy and self-determination, our still valid form of government, freedom, and furthermore they facilitated long-lasting peace and its resulting prosperity.

Tired of war and with the dearest wish for peace and quiet, people in the defeated and destroyed Germany were glad about the end of war. Shaped by an identical western cultural sphere – with the same existing values, a similar character, a religion in common and the same interests – this enormous recovery could flourish hand in hand, and this democratization was able to succeed.

My generation suffered at the front to the largest part involuntarily and without good reason – in constant fear of death, the daily horrors in front of our eyes. Yet neither we nor the generations of our children, grandchildren and great-grandchildren are guilty of this crime.

That we always remember history, especially our own, and learn from its fatal mistakes is self-evident and proper. The look at the injustice of the past, however, ought not to block our view of the injustice of today, but ought to raise our awareness for our responsibility in our own country and all over the world.

Therefore history ought to be viewed with constant involvement and in an objective manner, most of all with proper prudence.

May all future generations be spared for all eternity such experiences and events as they happened then.

In Memoriam

'Gott mit uns', 'God with us', was the legend on the metal belt buckles we Wehrmacht soldiers wore. I belonged to those fortunate whom God did not abandon in their need and who were allowed to return home.

Yet more than five million of my comrades never saw their home again.

This book is dedicated to them, too, and to the more than a million civilians killed, to the thirteen million expellees and to the victims of the other countries involved in this war.